HausMagick

HausMagick

Transform Your Home
with Witchcraft

Erica Feldmann

HarperOne
An Imprint of HarperCollinsPublishers

HarperOne

HarperCollins books may be purchased for educational, business, or sales promotional use. For information, please email the Special Markets Department at SPsales@harpercollins.com.

Originally published as *HausMagick* in The United Kingdom in 2019 by Penguin Random House UK. First HarperOne hardcover published in 2019. Published by arrangement with Ebury Press, a division of the Random House Group Limited.

FIRST EDITION

Photography © Erica Feldmann, 2018
With the exception of the photography that appears on: pages 8–9, 28–29, 158, and 221 © Winnie Man, 2018; and page 247 © Dave Wells, 2018.
Illustrations © Erika Leahey, 2018

Library of Congress Cataloging-in-Publication Data

Names: Feldmann, Erica, 1982-author.
Title: Hausmagick : transform your home with witchcraft / Erica Feldmann.
Description: FIRST EDITION. | San Francisco : HarperOne, 2019. | Includes index.
Identifiers: LCCN 2018036758 (print) | LCCN 2018044413 (ebook) | ISBN 9780062906168 (e-book) | ISBN 9780062906151 (hardcover)
Subjects: LCSH: Magic. | Home—Miscellanea. | Households—Miscellanea. | Witchcraft.
Classification: LCC BF1623.H67 (ebook) | LCC BF1623.H67 F45 2019 (print) | DDC 133.4/3—dc23
LC record available at https://lccn.loc.gov/2018036758

19 20 21 22 23   WOR   10 9 8 7 6 5 4 3 2 1

I dedicate this book to my dad.

(And to all the people who put up with me while I wrote it.)

CONTENTS

INTRODUCTION

Hi, welcome to *HausMagick!*

When I first began writing about interiors I struggled to find my voice amid the multitude of aspirational books, blogs, and magazines offering tips and tricks, DIY tutorials, craft projects, and trend reports. While I loved all of those things, I soon realized that I was interested in the essential ingredients that make a space both look and feel good at the same time. How to efficiently harness the magic that makes a house feel like a home, without spending a lot of money. I've learned that what most homes are missing isn't a beautiful sofa or the perfect decor: it's simply the intention to make them feel special. That is why my company, HausWitch, was created. HausWitch is about giving people the tools to heal their spaces, love their homes, and save their money. This book is one of those tools. It is a spell book of interior alchemy. It is about joining the astral plane and the material world to help you transform the energy in your home.

Being fully comfortable in your home is a legitimately important part of self-care and is central to the HausWitch mission. But I believe there are two types of comfort: the kind that helps you to relax, restore, and align with your higher self, and the kind that isolates you from the world around you, lulling you into complacency. That second kind of comfort comes from things like unlimited cable channels, screen culture, and cheap consumer goods. Now, don't get me wrong; I'm no stranger to the luxury of ordering things

online from the comfort of my couch. But it is when you are deeply connected to your space that you feel truly comfortable within it. My goal for this book is to help you to develop that connection in an authentic and meaningful way.

Even if you don't consider yourself a homebody, at the very least your home is a shelter. In the storm of our chaotic, anxiety-producing world, it provides a retreat where you can recharge your batteries, fill up your cup, or simply get a decent night's sleep. In terms of self-care, this stuff is right up there with eating well and exercising. By practicing a little HausMagick, you're honoring your home for the important role it plays in your life.

HausMagick will guide you through the key ways I believe you can harness the positive energy in your home. Over the years, I've worked with a range of experts— from interior designers and antique dealers to makers, artists, and, of course, witches. Combining their creative knowledge with my own personal study of earth magic, astrology, tarot, and energy work, I've crafted this magical instruction manual for you. Each field of wisdom aims to achieve balanced energy in various areas of life, which will allow you to live in harmony with yourself and nature—and that includes the energy of your home.

With these practices in mind, I want to help you improve six fundamental elements I believe make a living space into a home: manifestation, clearing, protection, comfort, harmony, and balance.

Even if you don't fully ascribe to the metaphysical philosophies in this book, I hope to show you how much you can benefit from incorporating elements of them into your daily life and home style in simple ways that work for you.

What Is HausMagick?

Like a lot of people, I suffered from anxiety growing up, and sometimes still do. As a sensitive and empathic child, the world could feel very overwhelming to me at times. One of the ways I was able to feel like I had some power over my circumstances was by connecting to the spaces I was in. I was often too shy to speak to the people around me, but I seemed to be able to communicate with the room itself. I could just feel it. This makes perfect sense to me now, because I know that spaces are filled with energy, as are the objects within them. By tapping into that energy, I was able to feel rooted and safe when I was anxious.

Soon enough, what started as a coping mechanism became a hobby. Relatives would call me in to consult on a room or an office that no one liked to be in. I would show them how to rearrange the art on the wall or the furniture to improve the quality of the space. It was just something I could sense naturally. I was a perfect candidate for a future in interior design.

But I am a person who insists on doing things the hard way, so rather than going to interior design school and immediately starting a career I enjoyed, I decided instead to get a degree in history, and then another in Witches (well, technically my degree is in Gender and Cultural Studies, but my research concentration was Witches)—and only then did I start a home-decorating business!

Throughout my twenties, I became obsessed with interior design blogs. I loved that home decorating wasn't just for those who could afford to hire fancy designers anymore. An explosion of accessible, design-oriented blogs full of DIY ideas aimed at everyone appeared out of nowhere. I soaked it all up. I read at least four to five of them daily. I learned about lighting concepts, furniture design, how to distinguish between one hundred different shades of white paint—you name it, there was a blog post about it.

As grateful as I was to get a free education in practical, contemporary interior design, I also felt alienated by posts about "budget makeovers," where the budget was still completely inaccessible to me and the people I knew. As frustrating as that was, it pushed me to get creative. I realized that if I wanted to create an environment that looked and felt good enough to be photographed for a glossy magazine, while not costing a fortune, I would have to get crafty . . . witchcrafty that is. (Sorry, I can't pass up an opportunity for a good pun.)

Initially, the witch part of HausWitch had more to do with my own personal identification with the word "witch," and the idea that a "magical" (i.e., inexpensive) transformation would occur in the room I was making over. Without a lot of money, the revamp would have to come from repurposing the home's existing decor, refinished old furniture, and DIY projects.

As a teenager, I had dabbled in Wicca (a goddess-based religion that uses earth magic as its spiritual practice) by casting love spells in my bedroom at night. I quickly became discouraged by my lack of access to the "necessary" tools for practicing spells (try finding exotic herbs in a suburban mall or leaving the house at midnight to light a bonfire without your parents knowing) and gave up on Wicca.

It was only when my dear friend Kaitlyn, who had recently moved across the country, asked me to cast a spell to help her find a new house that I really returned to magic. I hadn't practiced magic in years, but, because it was a home-related request, it felt natural, and I crafted a spell with ease. (More on that in Chapter 1, Manifesting.)

That night, as I was going to bed, an idea hit me like a lightning bolt: "Why don't I put together little house-spells for my clients to bring good energy into their homes? No— why don't I make little house-spells for everyone!" I didn't get much sleep that night because I just kept channeling ideas. At that point, I had a very basic knowledge of space healing, things like burning sage to clear a space and fake plants being bad Feng Shui, but I became obsessed with knowing more. I devoured books on practical magic, Jungian psychology of the home, working with crystals, and energy healing. I knew I was onto something, and it was the best feeling in the world.

In November of the same year, I launched HausCraft— six different spells (packaged in the cutest tiny house-shaped boxes) for bringing different types of good vibes into your home. I wanted them to be different from other witchcraft spell kits I'd seen: friendlier and more welcoming for people who had never thought about practicing magic before. The kits are based on the same principles as the chapters of this book—manifestation, clearing, comfort, protection, harmony, and balance. They were an instant hit. And that's when I started dreaming bigger.

A year later, HausCraft was a full-time job on its own. I had some money in savings from when my beloved father passed away but no idea what to do with it, and I didn't know how I could ever fully support myself with HausWitch. (I will say that, since the beginning, my amazing clairvoyant, Christopher, always insisted that HausWitch would be my career, even when I had no idea how it would happen.) That's when another lightning bolt hit me and I heard a spirit guide whisper, "You know what you want is to open a store."

The store I had in mind would be like a giant HausCraft spell kit. It would carry all the things you need to make your home feel incredible and smell fantastic.

I knew the store had to be in Salem, Massachusetts, where I had lived and studied a few years earlier. The first retail space I looked at was in the middle of downtown "Witch City" and I realized the second I walked in that I was opening a store and it was going to be there.

My business, HausWitch Home + Healing, has been a total dream come true. All different kinds of magical practitioners, energy workers, and kindred spirits come to the store, and we have created an awesome community of like-minded people. Some of my closest friends, whom I refer to as my coven, have given the store its true heart and soul, and you will hear from many of them in the pages of this book. It often seems like we were destined to find each other, to work together, support each other, and make magic together. It taught this introverted Haus-cat how rewarding it can be to be a part of a community.

The way all of these pieces fell into place has informed the way I practice magic in a profound way. If you're trying to manifest something that just isn't in the best interest of your highest self and your true soul path, no amount of magic spells will bring it to you. But if you leave yourself open to the flow, synchronicity, and—yes—the magic of the universe, dreams you never even knew you had can come true.

WITCHING 101

Am I a witch? The short answer is yes! The longer answer is that I like to say that I have always liked the acronym W.I.T.C.H.—for "Woman in Total Control of Herself," which is something I strive very hard to be. As a feminist, I believe that the witch is an amazing archetype for channeling the innate and often unseen power of the divine feminine. To me, the word "witch" represents all that has been oppressed by patriarchy, and using the title today is a reclaiming of it.

THERE ARE AS MANY DEFINITIONS OF WHAT BEING A WITCH MEANS AS THERE ARE PRACTITIONERS AND BELIEVERS.

Every witch sees herself differently, but I believe that what unites us is the effort to stay centered and grounded in our energy so that we can use our inner strength to manifest the things that we want to bring into our lives and the world around us.

In terms of the spiritual side of my magical practice, I adhere to a New Age sensibility, which puts working with energy at the forefront of everything.

Everything Is Energy, and Energy Is Everything

A New Age lifestyle and its system of knowledge are meant to connect believers with the wider, natural world and put our lives on earth into a context that promotes an intentional existence that is aligned with nature.

Since becoming conscious of how much mindful living, intention-setting, and manifesting can change my life, I have seen my own happiness and sense of well-being increase dramatically. I feel more empowered and supported in my everyday life, and I am more able to act as a support for others and the planet.

Now, here's the best part: living this way does not mean that you have to start using crystal balls or dancing naked in the woods (although you could!). It means taking simple steps toward improving your quality of life and starting to see how you can shift the energy around you in your favor.

VIBES

When witches talk about "good vibes" or "bad vibes," what we are referring to is the fact that every single thing on earth and in your home—from crystals and plants to furniture, people, pets, walls, herbs, objects, and even emotions—runs at its own individual vibrational frequency. This is just basic science; everything is made of atoms, and atoms are always moving, creating a vibrational frequency.

Working with vibrations is how you work with energy. By paying thoughtful attention to the vibrations that you bring into your space, you affect the overall energy. Perhaps you can imagine the difference in vibration between, say, a ceramic bowl crafted by hand, with the thoughtfulness and attention of the maker infused right into its makeup, versus a mass-produced item made of plastic by a machine. Building an awareness of how different vibrations function in your space is a major theme of this book.

Basic Witching

As you'll see, many types of magical techniques complement each other, and there is a lot to be gained by understanding the basics of each and how they relate to one another.

Don't get too carried away with having the "right" magical things around you. Think of it this way: a spell is a prayer with props. Use whatever tools help you to best communicate your intentions to the world. Witchcraft is all about self-empowerment, so remember you are the magic behind your spells.

I use a multidisciplinary approach that incorporates different types of magical philosophies drawn from all corners of the world. Here is an introduction to a few of them so you'll have a nice working knowledge of certain key ideas and terms when we explore the larger themes of manifestation, clearing, comfort, protection, harmony, and balance in your home.

A Note about New Age Cultural Appropriation

While writing this book, I have grappled with the ways in which I have culturally appropriated elements of my magical practice from religious and spiritual cultures that are not my own. By cultural appropriation, I mean when a dominant culture adopts practices belonging to another. This happens in New Age circles all the time, as we draw on traditions from Hinduism, Buddhism, and Native American Shamanism (to name just a few), often without properly understanding the entirety of these complex belief systems.

So how do we practice a more responsible witchcraft? By self-educating, even if it makes us feel uncomfortable, because that encourages us to remain open, have conversations, and listen to voices that have been silenced. By doing this, we start the project of cultural appreciation rather than appropriation, familiarize ourselves with the roots of our spiritual practices, and use them with respect and reverence for the communities from which they came.

Moving forward, we need to understand the right ways of incorporating the healing practices of other cultures into our society, where they are so badly needed, without distorting or appropriating them. I believe that as witches, we have a duty to set an example of how this can be done. To that end, I have included a few resources in the Recommended Reading section to help you understand these practices within their original context.

THE FIVE MOON PHASES

Working with the phases of the moon is a great way to align with cosmic timing. It's important to be in sync with the lunar cycles since the moon's proximity to earth makes its impact felt on us more than any other celestial body, aside from the sun.

Working with the moon phases is, moreover, simple to do because there are only five main phases that are important for spell work. You can use this primer to time anything from casting a manifestation spell to cleaning your house or planting a garden!

NEW MOON: in magical practices, the new moon is held to be that first sliver, that skinniest little fingernail crescent which shows up in the sky after a few days of darkness. It's the beginning of the moon cycle and is the best time to welcome in a fresh start, set intentions, and plant seeds (literal or symbolic).

WAXING MOON: when the moon is said to be waxing, the visible part of the moon is growing in the sky. This is the best time for manifesting spells and drawing things to you—like that shiny new apartment for which you've just spotted a listing. Think of what you want more of in your life right now. The waxing moon is all about amplification, attraction, and expansion.

FULL MOON: the full moon is the time for welcoming any kind of positivity into your life. It is a time of celebration, completion, abundance, and gratitude. Not only is it a great time to appreciate all that was brought in during the waxing phase, but it's a great time to feel your full power. Throw your housewarming party on the full moon for guaranteed high vibes.

WANING MOON: the moon is getting smaller in the sky, so this is a good time for letting go of what you want less of in your life. Now would be the time for decluttering and cleaning out closets (literally and symbolically). Have a yard sale or donate unused items to charity.

DARK MOON: for three days before the new moon, the moon is not visible in the sky. This is the perfect time for space clearing, banishing negative energies, and releasing what's no longer serving you. Like, say, that piece of art your mother gave you that you secretly hate. The key words here are "Let it go."

While it's important to align with the moon phases, don't feel discouraged if you are having trouble coordinating your intention-setting with the right moon phase; just try to frame your intention differently. If, for example, you want to do a manifesting spell but the moon is waning or dark, you can make it a spell about removing obstacles that stand in the way of getting what you want. And it can work both ways. If you want to release something while the moon is waxing, visualize what your life will look and feel like after you've released it and draw that energy in.

BALANCING ENERGIES

As we'll discover throughout this book, the concept of balance is key to creating decor that nurtures you, mind, body, and spirit. There are a couple of different frameworks that I find useful for bringing in balance, and which draw on some of the oldest and most foundational ways in which humans have conceptualized the world around them.

YIN AND YANG: throughout history, humans have divided the world into all sorts of binary oppositions, such as Male/Female, Day/Night, etc. This is illustrated perfectly in Chinese philosophy by the symbol of the Yin and Yang. You've probably seen the symbol of the Yin and Yang used in countless contexts: the circle split down the middle to form two equal paisley shapes, one black and one white. Each side has a smaller circle within it of the opposite color to show that one should not exist without the other. It symbolizes the balance of the two essential energies of the universe: Yin energy, which is passive and associated with the moon, night, the feminine, death, slowness, and dark; and Yang energy, its complement and opposite, associated with action, the sun, daytime, the masculine, birth, speed, and light. (It is worth noting here that when using terms like "feminine" and "masculine," we are not talking about anything related to human gender identity or anatomy. It's simply a way of characterizing the two types of energy that society has matched to a particular gender.) This idea of balancing Yin and Yang energies runs through most New Age magical practices and is expressed in many different forms.

THE FOUR ELEMENTS: another useful framework for understanding how to balance energies is through the four elements—earth, air, fire, and water—which are considered

to be the foundations of all matter in the universe. Many modern-day witchcraft practices call on these elemental energies heavily, invoking them as a way to align ceremonies and rituals with the natural world. Different divinatory practices such as the tarot and astrology use the four elements as categories which relate to the card suits and the different zodiac signs. For example, the twelve zodiac signs are divided up so that three signs fall in each of the elemental categories: I am a Gemini, for instance, which is an air sign, as are Libra and Aquarius; whereas Aries, Sagittarius, and Leo are all fire signs; Pisces, Cancer, and Scorpio are water signs; and Capricorn, Taurus, and Virgo are earth signs.

Fire energy is all about action and change. It's a good energy for shaking things up. Creativity, passion, and sexuality are all charged with fire. Earth is grounding and stabilizing, and connects us to the material world. Air is all about intellectual thought, mental focus, and precision. Finally, water invokes emotion, creativity, and flow. Spirit, or aether, is considered the fifth element. I believe that the intention you are setting to connect with universal energy relates to the spirit element of any spell.

CRYSTAL HEALING

Now for the sparkly part! Throughout the rest of this book I'll be dropping the names of crystals like they're celebrities, and we'll get more into the healing properties of each as we go. In the meantime, let's talk about some ways of working with crystals that are simple and effective.

Cultures from the beginning of recorded history, all across the globe, have recognized the energetic medicine of crystals and minerals. As early as 1151, Hildegard of Bingen (the Benedictine Abbess, artist, mystic, author, composer) wrote extensively about gems like topaz, jasper, and amethyst in her book *Physica*—one of the earliest works on Western herbal medicine to be written by a woman. Of agate, she writes: "Its nature will make [a] person capable, judicious, and prudent in speech, because it is born from fire and air and water."

Crystals form deep within the earth, and each different one holds its own unique vibration. The healing power of crystals comes from the ability of these vibrations to connect the user to the earth and to harmonize with the healing energies of the natural world. For more on the science of crystal healing, see page 38.

Crystals come in all different sizes and forms. A "raw" crystal is one with rough edges that hasn't been shaped, polished, or carved. A "tumbled" stone has been put in a rock tumbler with an abrasive grit and water for a long time until all of the rough edges are smooth (these are great for slipping into your pocket to carry with you). Finally, a "carved" crystal has been cut into a specific shape meant to enhance the look and feel of the stone, and to make it easier to use. For example, many crystals end up carved into a shape where one end is flat and the other is a sharp point. This is called a crystal point (makes sense, right?), and that shape makes it easier to display.

THE SCIENCE OF
CRYSTAL HEALING

I'm blessed to have witches in so many different walks of life in my community. Here, Shaina Cohen and Michaela Zullo, trained geologists and energy workers, explain the science behind the healing magic of crystals:

The scientific study of crystals and their formation is known as crystallography. All minerals are crystalline solids, which means their atoms are arranged in a highly ordered microscopic structure that repeats indefinitely in all directions (known as a "crystal lattice"). As a crystal grows and becomes visible to the human eye, its appearance reflects its microscopic structure—which is why crystals take on a wide variety of shapes, including sheets, cubes, and points.

In order to describe the science behind the healing potential of crystals, let's take quartz as an example. All quartz crystals are made of a molecule known as silicon dioxide (SiO_2). The individual atoms of silicon and oxygen in the crystal lattice of quartz are bonded together (through interatomic forces). Although bonded together, they are in constant motion—each atom and its associated bonds all vibrate at unique frequencies. These frequencies determine how any given crystalline solid resonates.

Now, let's consider a wristwatch that keeps time using a quartz crystal. The quartz crystal vibrates at a known frequency, which allows quartz clocks to keep time more precisely than other mechanisms. This is only possible because quartz is a piezoelectric mineral. Minerals with this physical property can transmit energy in the form of electricity as a result of both the chemical composition and the atomic structure of the crystal. All crystals are characterized by unique physical properties (and unique vibrations) that control the way they interact with the world around them.

This example, our ability to keep time precisely using the vibrations of quartz, sheds light on how the physical mechanisms of this reality (even those we cannot see) can have different, tangible effects on our lives.

The easiest way to bring crystals into your home is to place a crystal in a conspicuous place in your living space according to its healing properties. For example, amethyst is perfect for a bedside table as it helps with sleep by making you feel safe and supported. Similarly, I always have pyrite on my desk because it's good for willpower and manifestation.

Next to working directly with the crystal itself, the easiest option is to make a crystal essence. An essence is an elixir that holds the vibration of a stone or mineral and preserves it in a water/alcohol mixture. In this liquid form, you can access the healing power of any crystal by using a few drops of its essence. For example, you can ingest it by putting a few drops of the essence directly on your tongue or by diluting them in drinking water. You can also use them topically by dabbing your skin with drops or adding essences to skincare and beauty products. Or you can create some pretty magical room sprays and cleaning products, as I'll be showing you how to do during our journey together.

HOW TO CREATE A CRYSTAL ESSENCE POTION

1

Cleanse your crystal. If you've just brought your
new crystal friend home with you, or it's been with you for
a while, you may want to cleanse your crystal before using
it. This is super simple: you can just hold it under clear
running water, clear it with sage smoke (see page 89), or
place it in sunlight for a half hour or so. You can also place
it in a bowl of salt for a few minutes. This will get rid of any
of the random energy your stone may have sucked up, so
that you can reset it to your intended frequency.

2

Set the intention. Sit for a minute with the crystal in
your dominant hand. Think about how you want this
crystal to help you. What are you hoping its healing
properties can aid you in? Close your eyes and really
visualize your intention in a way that feels right to you.

3

Place the crystal in or beside a clear glass of clean water—
no plastic, please, as this will not hold the vibrations as well!
(Also note that some stones are water soluble and
will start to dissolve when soaked in water.) Position this
and a small dropper bottle, in which to store your finished
essence, in direct sunlight for about four hours.

4

Fill your dropper bottle halfway with brandy and
the other half with the water from the glass. That's it!
You've got yourself a gem essence.

CHARGING OBJECTS

When working with magical objects it is important to "charge" them. This means infusing the object with a specific energy. Sometimes that energy is an intention you are setting. To do this, hold the object in your hand, or, if it's big, simply touch it, close your eyes, and meditate on the intention you would like it to have. For example, you could charge a souvenir you got on vacation with the energy of the fun and adventure you experienced on the trip. This means that when you go home, you are bringing that particular energy with you in physical form.

You can also charge objects with the cosmic energy of the sun or the moon. For example, I sometimes like to charge my crystals with moonlight by placing them on a windowsill under the full moon. This infuses them with the energy of abundance and gratitude, so that I can always have that energy around me.

10 OF PENTACLES

19 · THE SUN

7 OF WANDS

ASTROLOGY

The study of astrology goes way beyond checking your horoscope in the Sunday paper. Astrology connects what happens here on earth with what is happening in the sky above us. The stars, planets, and asteroids are all part of the natural world, and just because they are very far away does not mean they don't have an influence on your life. Try thinking of it like a cosmic map. Your birth chart, or the placement of heavenly bodies on the day you were born, is where you're coming from; and the way in which those same heavenly bodies move around the sky during your life signifies where you're going. For example, many people experience some disruption or upheaval in their lives between the ages of twenty-five and thirty. This coincides with your "Saturn Return," which is when planetary heavyweight Saturn returns to the same position it was in on the day you were born.

For our purposes, we'll be focusing on a part of astrology called "the houses," which are a feature of your birth chart. We'll get into that in more detail in Chapter 1, Manifesting.

TAROT

A typical tarot deck has seventy-eight cards, and most of those cards are much like a regular deck of playing cards, only with the four suits representing the four elements: pentacles/earth, cups/water, wands/fire and swords/air. There are fourteen cards per suit, which run from the ace through to the king. Those fifty-six cards are called the Minor Arcana. So, at first glance, the tarot is really not so different from the playing cards you used to play gin rummy with your nana.

Then there's the cards that go beyond a regular deck of playing cards: the Major Arcana. These twenty-two cards span from the Fool to the World. Despite how mysterious that may sound, you'll probably recognize these too, even if you've never picked up a tarot deck. They're the universal archetypes, the characters that we see over and over again in stories across different cultures, places, and time periods, and which appear in novels, movies, plays, and even in our own lives. Like all of our favorite characters, the Fool is on a journey, only they are traveling through the Major Arcana—from naïve beginnings all the way through to a joyful completion that brings together everything learned along the way.

We can look at our lives like this: a constant cycle of learning and growing through different life stages. Not all of those stages are easy, and some of them may even seem scary, like those symbolized by the Devil card. But even the Devil is just a temporary stage that involves working through any patterns, obsessions, and addictions that may stand in the way of you living your most aligned life.

HERBALISM

Plants are an integral part of the earth's ecosystem and a powerful part of any witch's tool kit. Besides the medicinal benefits, herbs carry their own magic. Each herb has very real and tangible effects on the body, and can also help represent themes, archetypes, and intentions in spell work.

Herbalism incorporates tinctures, teas, baths, and all sorts of herbal recipes. Whether you're using herbs for magic or medicine, it's always important to double check that whatever you're doing with herbs is safe. Confirm that there are no contraindications with any medicines that you might be taking if you plan on ingesting or coming into direct contact with plant matter. The recipes in this book include dried and fresh plants, essential oils, and essences. Essential oils are a very concentrated form of the plants, so it's a good idea to dilute them before putting drops directly on your skin. Flower and herbal essences capture the vibrational qualities of the herbs and do not actually include the plant matter itself. Think of these as being like an energetic medicine. Herbal bundles can include pieces of the plants and essential oils, and are generally placed around the home.

If you're interested in digging deep into herbalism, there are plenty of books and online courses available to expand your herbal knowledge and complement your magical practice.

Hopefully, by now you can see how all of these different tools are interrelated and can be combined to work together.

In the following chapters we'll weave together the magical practices that we've just learned about here through the six essentials for creating an intentional home that I mentioned earlier. We'll start with some manifesting magic to help you get clear about what you want your home to be like and how to achieve this. Then we'll give your space a nice fresh start by clearing some clutter and getting rid of stale, stuck energy. Protection is next, grounding yourself and guarding your home from ghosts, bad vibes, and the heebie-jeebies. Then it's time to get comfy in Chapter 4. We'll talk about how to make your space feel cozy by engaging all SIX senses. Chapter 5, on Harmony, will focus on living with others, blending decorating styles, and establishing healthy boundaries. Lastly, once all of the other pieces are in place, we'll relax into serenity and balance with plant magic and breathwork.

CHAPTER 1

MANIFESTING

Back when my friends Kaitlyn and Ben asked me for a spell to help them find the home of their dreams, what they were really asking for was a manifesting spell. For me, manifesting is an art form. It's the art of getting clear about what you want, setting an intention, and then opening yourself up to accept its fulfillment. Now, don't get me wrong, you don't always get what you want, but in the timeless words of Mick Jagger, you get what you need. Basically, the universe always knows best. Sometimes what we think we want isn't actually in our highest and best interest, and a huge part of manifesting is having that faith and trust in your higher power (however you name it—god/goddess, the universe, Spirit, etc.) to know what's actually in alignment for you. Human beings rooted in the material world aren't always privy to the grand plan.

Kaitlyn and Ben were very clear about what they needed, and they had been searching for a new home for a long time. I simply drew a rough outline of a house (coincidentally foreshadowing my brand's logo a short while later) and wrote their names in it. Then I placed a couple of crystals that I knew were good for manifesting success on top, along with a cozy-scented candle, and a magnet to attract the manifestation of their wishes. I snapped a picture of the whole thing and sent it to Kaitlyn.

"The witches are on it!" I wrote in a text message. Two weeks later, after months of searching, Kaitlyn and Ben moved into their dream house.

All I really did for them was focus that intention in such a way that the universe took notice. The spell helped them feel supported because they were trusting in a power bigger than themselves. It actually did the same for me. That night, my spell kits were born.

One of the keys to manifesting is to be as clear as possible about what it is that you actually want. There are several different techniques that I like to use for gaining clarity in order to set intentions.

VISION BOARDS

Vision boards are a widely used manifestation tool that have become very popular over the last decade or so. The idea is to help you become more aware of your most authentic desires by tapping into your unconscious mind through imagery and words. If you've never made one, the process is pretty simple. You collect photos, advertisements, newspaper clippings, fabric swatches, tarot cards, stickers, etc. that you respond to in a positive manner, and then arrange them on a wall or poster board in a thoughtful way.

For example, if I were making a "Dream House" vision board, I would cut out pictures from some home-design magazines, estate agent ads, furniture catalogs, and, maybe, some color samples or other home-related items that represent what I want my home to look and feel like. I would use some nice craft materials and mindfully curate the way the items look together.

Don't limit yourself when you're first gathering your materials; you can pare down and hone in when you're ready to put it all together. The way you choose to arrange your board and the intention behind it is like casting a spell.

Japanese washi tape is an awesome tool because it comes in a lot of different colors and patterns, and it sticks to paper and walls without damaging them.

There's more to making a vision board than simply collaging photos of aspirational images onto a poster board. A vision board alone will not bring a celebrity mansion into your life if you aren't already a millionaire. But it can help you to learn what really lights you up, and that self-knowledge is the first step toward manifesting a life that is rewarding and authentic to you.

KEYS

I love using old keys as a magical tool. What could be a better talisman for manifesting than a literal door opener? Charge a key with your intention and then use it to unlock the power of the universe!

Make sure to cleanse the key's energy before you use it for the first time—and again if you plan to reuse it for a different spell further down the line—by putting it in a bowl of salt for a few hours or running it through some sage smoke (see page 89). In the context of manifesting a new home, I would meditate on my intention while holding the key in my hand. Then I'd put it on my regular key chain and carry it with me at all times, or put it in my pocket while I'm house hunting.

Key spells can be useful in any situation in which you are trying to open yourself up to the right opportunity.

CRYSTALS FOR MANIFESTING

LABRADORITE

This stone is sometimes referred to as the "aurora stone," because when held in light, its blue-green shimmer is reminiscent of the Aurora Borealis, the northern lights. Placing labradorite on your third eye (see page 190) will help you to connect the dots and recognize synchronicities in your life, which will bring you into flow and alignment with the universe. This alignment will help you find your truest path and is crucial for manifesting your dreams into reality.

SMOKY QUARTZ

This stone's grounding properties help to bring your desires out of the ethereal plane and into the material world. Once your dreams or ideas are made conscious, smoky quartz can assist in organization and pragmatism. It is also a very protective crystal, so once you've manifested your intentions, smoky quartz will block any negative energies or influences that may try to get in the way.

PYRITE

I call pyrite the "get stuff done" stone. It's my all-time favorite because of its manifesting powers. Also known as fool's gold, pyrite forms in perfect cubes of all sizes, and its name comes from *pyr*, the Greek word for "fire." Think of pyrite as a spark of confidence that connects to your willpower, ambition, and persistence. After all, when you're manifesting you can't leave all the heavy lifting up to the universe. Pyrite will help you to show up for your higher self and create your own reality.

Labradorite

Smoky quartz

Pyrite

"PYRITE IT DOWN"
MANIFESTING SPELL

Don't let the cheeky name fool you—this simple spell
is a powerhouse of manifesting potential.

1

Write down or create a mini–vision board of whatever
it is you wish to manifest.

2

Place the paper on a flat and stable surface
near an open window.

3

Put a piece of pyrite, a candle, and an object that represents
the way opening for you (such as a key) on the paper.

4

Holding a piece of cone or stick incense in your hand,
visualize what it would look and feel like to have
what you desire. Try to be as detailed as possible in
your mind. Engage all of your senses.

5

Say, "Here is how I manifest what is in my highest and best."

6

Light the incense and place it on a fire-safe dish on your
paper. As the smoke flows out of the open window, imagine
your intention flowing out of your space and into the world.

WRITTEN IN THE STARS: FINDING YOUR FOURTH HOUSE

Another way to gain insight into what you truly want and need from your home is to look at your astrological birth chart. You may already be familiar with your zodiac sign, which is where the sun was in the sky when you were born, but there are plenty of other heavenly bodies in the sky, and they all have different traits associated with them. Your birth chart will ideally show where all of the planets (and some asteroids!) were in the sky at the exact minute of your birth. Knowing where the heavenly bodies were when you were born can give you an awareness of all sorts of different aspects of your life path and your personality. (It's easy and free to look up your birth chart on the internet on sites like www.astro.com; all you need is your birth date, exact time and place.) You'll get something that looks like this:

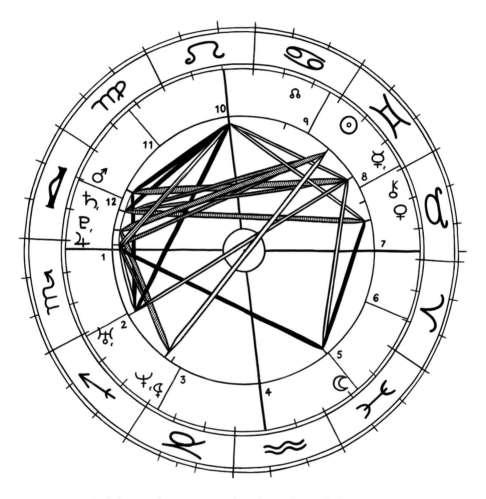

Isn't it crazy how even my chart has a "Haus" shape in it?!

Your birth chart is divided into twelve sections called houses. You should see little numbers in each section all around your chart: these relate to the houses. Each house represents a different area of your life, such as love, family or work, etc. For our purposes, we'll be focusing on the planets that are in your fourth house. The fourth house is all about home and what that means to you. It's also about family and emotions and how all of those things connect for you.

Come along on a journey to the stars with me, aided and abetted by my brilliant friend the astrologer Grace Harrington Murdoch, as we dive into an overview of what it means to have each of the following planets resident in your fourth house:

SUN: you have a strong connection to your home and heritage, and like to show it off. Your roots are integral to your identity and you're very protective of them. If possible, you'll thrive in a large space that gives you room to grow and make memories with family and friends.

MOON: you feel deep emotions around the idea of home and feeling rooted. You might also be fickle about how your home looks and want to refresh and redecorate often. Let your home be your hobby and allow yourself to go deep into discovering what makes your house feel like home.

MERCURY: your home will be on your mind and often the subject of conversation, but you may also find comfort in a more nomadic lifestyle. You like to bring mental and educational activities into the home, and hosting social gatherings is important to you.

VENUS: you'll learn a lot about self-love through making your home beautiful. You'll take great pride in decorating it, collecting art and precious objects for others to admire. You'll want a space that has room to display your treasures.

MARS: fiercely independent, you like DIY projects and would probably love a home with several projects to sink your teeth into. In order to truly feel at home, you need a place in which to burn off excess energy, like an exercise room, garden, backyard, or swimming pool.

JUPITER: your home brings you a lot of joy and helps you to feel expansive. High ceilings or major square footage will feel great to you, as will having large collections to display, such as books or artifacts from your travels.

SATURN: you connect to your home through responsibility and crave a sense of stability, which can sometimes weigh you down. Making sure you have a place to relax and nurture yourself is important. Look for ways to share your domestic responsibilities wherever possible to lighten your load.

URANUS: you may understand home differently to how your family of origin did and feel a strong desire to come and go as you please. The word "root" is a foreign concept to you and you'll like moving around a lot. When/if you do settle in one place, your home will reflect a rebellious aesthetic. If you approach nesting as another new adventure, you'll thrive.

NEPTUNE: you may be a bit reclusive and see home as your "backstage" to the world. Setting up an altar, meditation room, or any kind of sacred space within your home will provide

a retreat from the world. You should put an emphasis on privacy in order to truly feel supported in your home.

PLUTO: you feel more attached to the land that you live on than your home itself. Decor may lean toward dark, mysterious, and sensual. You are comfortable with the shadow side of life and aren't afraid of the dark . . . but just make sure you have a few sources of natural light in your space for balance.

MOON SIGNS

It's totally okay if you don't see any planets in your fourth house, by the way. When any of your houses are empty, it just means that you aren't meant to focus on that aspect of your life in this lifetime. Maybe you mastered it in another lifetime, or maybe you've got other karmic stuff to deal with now. Either way, you can still get an idea of the nature of your relationship with your home by looking at your moon sign. Your moon sign is—you guessed it—the sign in which the moon was when you were born. The moon represents emotions, but it also has a maternal energy, which is how it relates to the home. It's about how you feel nurtured and cared for.

Here are some decorating tips for bringing your space into starry alignment.

ARIES: the keyword here is BOLD. Aries is a fire sign, and that brings a lot of Yang energy into the home. You probably love a lot of color and brightness. You may want to consider bringing in decor in blue and gray tones to cool down some of that fire so your home feels more balanced.

TAURUS: Taurus is ruled by Venus, the planet of beauty and love. Your home should feel lush and layered with things that you adore. The kind of place with amazing natural light, gorgeous art, and sprawling houseplants.

GEMINI: represented by the Twins, Gemini moon homes can have a split personality, and that's okay! Just make sure you can figure out how to blend your two different styles. It's almost like decorating for a couple who have different tastes: once you figure it out, your home will feel remarkably balanced with a distinct point of view.

CANCER: is the ultimate water sign, and the concept of home is very important here. Think of a hermit crab with her shell, always carrying her home with her. You'd love to live near the water, or to decorate your home with art and furnishings that represent water.

LEO: the show-off of the zodiac, Leo moons will think of home as a stage. You'll want a space where you can make your domestic life performative. Hosting big dinner parties, with elaborate courses, or having the prettiest garden or the brightest Christmas lights on the block will make you glow.

VIRGO: minimalism is attractive to you because of your tendency toward precision and perfectionism. Your refined taste should bring in only the most tasteful furnishings and art. Your home should support your need to be organized and clutter-free with plenty of storage furniture and/or closets.

LIBRA: bring balance to their homes easily. You'll want to put some energy into making sure all of the elements are represented so that your home feels harmonious. Without that, you can feel restless or uneasy. Relationships are important to you, so you make a great live-in partner or roommate.

SCORPIO: these moons are all about the underworld, and you feel most at home in a space that lets you feel that deep intensity. Just make sure you balance the dark colors you feel drawn to with windows that let in a little natural light—or at least have some whimsical decorative lighting.

SAGITTARIUS: another fire sign, so if your moon is placed here you'll love pops of color and bright spaces. Sagittarius is usually a sign that loves travel, so it will be important to honor this within your home. Displaying artifacts from trips or other cultures you admire will keep you from feeling tied down when you're at home.

CAPRICORN: having your moon in Capricorn means you have a taste for the finer things in life, and you appreciate a nice status symbol every so often. Bringing nature into your home is also important, because Capricorn is an earth sign. A beautiful garden or some jealousy-inducing landscaping will help you feel at home.

AQUARIUS: air signs like Aquarius are always a little zany and rebellious. Your tastes in decor will be bold and truly individual to your tastes. Make sure your home reflects this; don't try to conform to what's in style or trending at the moment. Consider finding a blank slate where you can really make it your own, or move to a place that you can renovate to your heart's desire.

PISCES: home is your sacred space. You need a place where you can feel both a connection to spirituality and deeply secure in your private life. You'll want a home where you can give yourself over to transcendent experiences like dancing, meditating, and dreaming.

Now that you're starting to discover how to manifest your dream home, and how to align your current space with your best intentions, it's time to clean out anything that's no longer serving you both energetically and physically.

CHAPTER 2

CLEARING

JOE MATT THE POOR BASTARD D&Q

SPENT MATT JOE D&Q

ASTERIOS POLYP DAVID MAZZUCCHELLI

A Connecticut Yankee In King Arthur's Court Chwast

THE CANTERBURY TALES CHWAST

DANTE'S DIVINE COMEDY

Masterpiece COMICS DRAWN AND QUARTERLY

MOOMIN: THE COMPLETE TOVE JANSSON COMIC STRIP D+Q

SUGAR SKULL PANTHEON BOOKS

XED OUT

AKIRA 1 OTOMO

ISLE OF JERUS

COLORS TRANSPORT / TRASPORTI

NORROW 6

CAHIERS D'ART

WWW

LUCKY PEACH
LUCKY PEACH ISSUE
LUCKY PEACH ISSUE 2 — SWEET SPOT FALL 2011
LUCKY PEACH
THE STREETFOOD ISSUE
LUCKY PEACH ISSUE 2 — SWEET SPOT FALL 2011

CHINA

ELEPHANT

ELEPHANT

THE BELIEVER

Robert Motherwell

Intimate Collaborations

JACKSON POLLOCK'S MURAL
THE TRANSITIONAL MOMENT

ILLUSTRATION NEXT

ALBERS AND MOHOLY-NAGY

Self-TAUGHT GENIUS

Cindy Sherman

ROBERT DAVIDSON

Spiral Keiichi Tanaami

THE ESSENTIAL DAVID SHRIGLEY

Eva Hesse

THE LOST ART OF WILLIAM STEIG

AMERICAN SURFACES STEPHEN SHORE

POLAROID BOOK TASCHEN

Abstract Expressionism MoMA

MONET'S YEARS AT GIVERNY

BALTHUS
BALTHUS CATS AND GIRLS

OVERKILL THE ART OF TOMER HANUKA

American

Opening up physical and energetic spaces in your home will allow you to think more clearly, relax more deeply, and create a more meaningful relationship between yourself and the things in your home that you really treasure. Spring cleaning is great, but I recommend a seasonal practice of decluttering, deep cleaning, and space clearing to keep your home fresh and clean on every level.

Clearing Clutter: The Dark before the Dawn

In today's world, the accumulation of *stuff* has become an addiction so deep rooted, we don't even notice it anymore. We fill our closets, our basements, even storage units located outside the home with everything from nostalgic memorabilia to junk that we just can't seem to part with. This addiction is not only harming the environment and exploitative of the people who make the cheap goods we consume, but it's also weighing us down physically, emotionally, and spiritually in our daily lives—and for what?

In my experience, most of what we store, i.e., the things we don't actually use on a regular basis, is useless excess. Out of sight, out of mind, right? Not really. Think of the things you have around your home. You're trying to relax and enjoy the space you've made for yourself, only to have your eye stop at that pile of papers on the desk or the old exercise bike you never use. Even if you're able to overlook these little messes in your conscious mind, your unconscious mind soaks it up—and that's where it becomes a problem.

While I was growing up, my family's home was relatively cluttered. Once a year or so, when my bedroom had become overrun with things, my mother and I would go through it all. It was, actually, fun. I didn't realize it at the time, but looking back, I can see that what made it more fun was, in part, because we were making the atmosphere in my room feel lighter by taking away *stuff*.

As an adult, I have always lived in apartments, and the good thing about small-space living is that it can force you to purge unused and unnecessary belongings more often. Some might argue that I border on the obsessive side when it comes to decluttering, but I assure you that if you look close enough, I too have piles of mail and unread books semi-discreetly tucked away. However, I know that whether I'm at home or in my store, I feel anxious, disorganized, and overwhelmed when I encounter clutter, and I find it harder to relax when I'm at home and harder to be productive when I'm at work.

There are a million reasons why we all hold on to *stuff*. Working out why, for yourself, can feel healing, but for our purposes all you need to know is that getting rid of some (or maybe a lot) of your *stuff* will make you feel a whole lot better.

STRATEGIES FOR PURGING

If you have not read *The Life-Changing Magic of Tidying Up*, I urge you to, because Marie Kondo is the expert when it comes to how to physically declutter your home. At the heart of Marie Kondo's method is the question: Does this object/book/article of clothing/etc. spark joy? If it doesn't, discard it.

The result is that you will be surrounded only by your most precious treasures, and they will have room to breathe and be enjoyed.

The method I use with my clients is to make three piles:

KEEP/DONATE/TRASH

Pick a room and go through everything. If you haven't used it or looked at it in six months, put it in the *DONATE* or *TRASH* pile. If you're putting it in the *KEEP* pile, ask yourself if it really feels special or if you're keeping it because you feel like you should.

I kept several large Tupperware boxes of "memories" or "life artifacts" for years. I lugged them around with me from apartment to apartment like dead weight: old school reports from elementary school, awards I won in sports, and old ill-fitting concert T-shirts I would never wear again. In my mind, I was keeping them as a record of who I am, thinking that maybe someday someone might be interested in seeing them.

However, I realized how falsely romanticized this idea was when my father passed away a few years ago. He left behind two homes completely packed with stuff. Yet everything of his that I cared about fit into a small backpack. I realized then that *stuff* doesn't matter as much as you think it does. I miss my father every single day. I think about all his *stuff* that I left behind exactly NEVER.

BANISHING *STUFF*
WITNESS SPELL

If you are ready to part with your stuff, including some
life artifacts, here is a spell you can perform to
honor them as you say good-bye. Perform this spell
on a day when the moon is waning or dark.

1

Light a white candle with a fresh smell. I like
something minty but maybe fresh flowers or
sweet vanilla feels better to you. All that matters is
that the scent feels fresh and clean.

2

Open at least one window in your space if possible.

3

Invite a close friend, partner, or family member to
sit with you and go through your life artifacts one by one.
They will act as a witness, allowing you to share
your memories with them, while detaching from the
objects that hold those memories.

4

Use the *KEEP/DONATE/TRASH* piles if that feels helpful.
Treat everything as a sacred object, even if you're getting
rid of it. Try to express gratitude for everything you're
throwing out. This can be a silent acknowledgment or
spoken out loud. For example, say the object is a trophy
from a sport you played as a kid: thank the trophy for
holding the memory of success and winning, and then allow
yourself to pull that feeling away from the object. Let it be
absorbed into your aura—and then release your attachment
to it. For objects that you're donating, see if you can set a
loving, positive intention for whoever receives the item next.

5

Condense the amount of artifacts that you keep to
about one-third (or less!) of what it was. Maybe
you can even put some of these treasures on display
in your home rather than keeping them in boxes?

6

Thank your witness for holding the space for you to process
and connect to your memories.

Energetic Clearing

Now that you've physically cleared your space of clutter, it's the perfect time to perform a space clearing to help cleanse it on an energetic level. Humans have used different methods for clearing energy for years—using smoke, hand clapping, rattles, or bells. Find out which method you prefer and find most effective by experimenting; the important thing is to find a method that works to clear the energy in your space on a regular basis, and especially after a big decluttering or deep cleaning.

A NOTE ON "SMUDGING"

Many Native American cultures "smudge," which involves
burning sage or other herbs that give off smoke
that contains healing properties. But the word "smudge"
describes a specific ritual, which is used as part of a
larger sacred ceremony. Therefore, the term "smudging"
should only really be used to describe the full
traditional Native American ritual.

HOLY SMOKE

Smoke represents the transmutation of the material world into the higher spirit realm. Herbs for clearing can come in a few different forms. The most common is a stick, a bundle of one herb or several tied together with string. You light the end of the stick and hold it almost like a magic wand. (Don't wave the burning stick around too much, though, because stray embers can fly off!) Use an abalone shell or fireproof dish to catch the ashes as you go. You can also burn loose herbs in the shell or dish by lighting a piece of charcoal and sprinkling herbs or resin on top. The important thing is to let the smoke fill the space by hitting every nook and cranny of it.

Before you clear your space, you should clear yourself so as to stop any negative or stuck energy from clinging to your physical or energetic body. You can also think of a simple mantra to repeat in your mind or say out loud in order to bring in positivity while clearing out negative energy. Something as simple as "I clear this space of any negative energy and replace it with my highest and best energy" works great.

Here are some of the most common herbs and plants used for clearing:

SAGE: by far the most well-known herb for space clearing, because it is strongly associated with purification. Many people believe that sage contains antibacterial properties and that the smoke literally cleans the air as the plant burns. It is a common practice to burn sage when moving into a new home to clear the previous owner's energy.

MUGWORT: Mugwort is a supermystical herb. When burned, mugwort can clear and protect the space from ghosts and welcome in psychic dreams.

CEDAR: will add some protection to your space when used for clearing. Cedar carries an ancient, masculine energy that will ground your space while clearing and raising the vibrations.

SWEETGRASS: instead of removing negative energy, sweetgrass brings in—well—sweetness. It comes in the form of a long braid and can be burned like incense in a dish, rather than moved around the space like a sage stick. It calls on ancestor energy and invites all of your most positive spirit guides into the space.

An important thing to remember about clearing with herbs such as sage is that the quality of the plant and your connection to it matter. If you aren't growing your own herbs for clearing, make sure your source harvests their herbs ethically and respectfully. Using herbs that are aligned with your own ancestral traditions or ones that are connected to the geographical area in which you live now is a great way to enhance your space-clearing efforts.

CLEARING SPRAY

Sometimes burning herbs to clear isn't an option. Maybe you live somewhere that doesn't allow flames, or you're worried you might cause chaos with the smoke alarms. No worries! Making a spray with sage essential oil is super easy and does the job nicely too.

INGREDIENTS

a small spray bottle
  (approx. 30 mL/2 fl. oz.)

sage essential oil

sage essence (optional)

other favorite essential
  oils (optional)

spring water

witch hazel

Charge an empty glass spray bottle on a sunny windowsill for a few hours.

Put a few drops of sage essential oil into the bottle. You can also add a few drops of a tincture made from sage essence, which can be found at many health food stores.

Feel free to add other essential oils for aromatherapy purposes. I like lavender and mint. Calm and clean.

Fill the bottle three-quarters of the way with spring water and the last quarter of the way with witch hazel. (Witch hazel acts as a preservative. You can also use vodka.)

Spray around your space in the same way you would clear with smoke!

USING SOUND TO CLEAR

In addition to using the sounds of bells or rattles, you can use your favorite music to clear your space of unwanted energy. Try blasting out your favorite song and dancing around your space to shake up stuck, stale energy, and to infuse some fun positive vibes. I like to use this method if I have had a negative experience with a guest and can feel their energy lingering around the place after they've left. It's a good way to get the energy moving again and infuse some of my personal energy back in.

CLEARING OBJECTS

You can energetically cleanse individual objects as well. Think of how much energy comes in with a new piece of furniture or decor. It will have the energy of whoever made it and whoever else may have touched it or considered buying it in the store, as well as the person who sold it. Consider the items you purchase from vintage or secondhand stores.

CAN YOU EVEN IMAGINE HOW MANY DIFFERENT ENERGIES ARE ATTACHED TO YOUR NEW FABULOUS VINTAGE CHAIR?

You can clear an object the same way you would clear a room, using any of the above methods.

CRYSTALS FOR CLEARING

Crystals are wonderful tools for energetic cleansing. Bring in crystals in cool tones like blues and greens to help clear the air for open communication, and use transparent or white stones to connect to your highest self.

APOPHYLLITE

This clear sparkler is perfect for enhancing psychic sight and intuition. Apophyllite is universal light in physical form. It holds some of the highest vibrations of any crystal and is used in many healing practices. It is extremely useful for clearing the energy of old emotional trauma from both the body and environment. Add a few drops of apophyllite essence to a room spray for an instant jolt of uplifting energy.

KYANITE

A unique crystal in that it doesn't hold any negative vibrations and therefore never needs to be cleansed or cleared. Its blue color connects it to the throat, making for ease and clarity in communication. Next time you need to have a tough conversation to "clear the air," keep a piece of kyanite in your pocket or hold one in your hand.

FLUORITE

An awesome crystal for home organization because it helps to discern between what is in your highest and best interests and what is no longer serving you; for instance, what you should keep and what you should donate or throw away. It cleanses your auric field, while helping you to focus on your true path in life.

Apophyllite   *Kyanite*

Fluorite

Natural Cleaning

Once you've purged the stuff that's no longer serving you, and cleared the energy, it's time to actually clean! Rather than using store-bought cleaning products, you can try mixing your own. They are kinder to the environment, toxin-free, and human- and pet-friendly.

When you make your own cleaning products you can infuse your personal intentions into them, create your own scents by blending essential oils, and even experiment with adding gem essences to make cleaning your home like casting a spell!

ALL-PURPOSE CLEANER

To make a 400 mL (14 fl. oz.) bottle of all-purpose cleaner, you'll need the following:

INGREDIENTS

30 g (1 oz.) Sals Suds (or Castile soap)

1 teaspoon borax

30 mL (1 fl. oz.) vodka

distilled water

essential oil(s) of your choice

Once you've gathered your ingredients, mix them together in a bowl.

Add five to twenty drops of essential oil for scent. (I like bergamot for a fresh citrus fragrance.)

Add to your bottle, using a funnel if necessary, and fill the rest with distilled water. If you also add a few drops of clearing crystal essence at this stage, it will take your cleaning spell to the next magical level.

FRESH AIR

At the end of the day, never underestimate the power of some fresh air. There is something so simple and healing about simply allowing outside air to circulate through your home. Use your windows like allies.

THEIR ABILITY TO BRING LIGHT, FRESH ENERGY INTO YOUR HOME, WHILE GIVING UNWANTED ENERGY A WAY TO ESCAPE, MAKES WINDOWS POWERFUL MAGICAL INSTRUMENTS.

I know that you will feel a sense of lightness and relief when your space has been cleaned and cleared, because coming home to a clean, clutter-free home is like taking a giant weight off your shoulders. Once you've done the heavy lifting of sorting through what's no longer serving you, it's time to protect your home from any negative influences that may try to sneak back in!

CHAPTER 3

PROTECTION

In European folk tales, the North Wind is characterized as a cantankerous yet helpful force of nature, helping a princess find her prince here, giving an impoverished child the means to feed his family there. Between the East, West, South, and North Winds, the North Wind was always the biggest, baddest, and most powerful.

I came to learn about the North Wind through an ornate, gothic-style chair in my parents' living room when I was a child. Slightly out of place in our mash-up of otherwise contemporary furnishings, the carved mahogany artifact had claws on its arms and legs and a ferocious face carved into the back. My mother told me it was the face of the North Wind.

In the late nineteenth century, during the Gothic Revival period of architecture and furniture design, German woodcarvers made their way into the workshops of Midwestern furniture makers in the States and brought their traditions and mythologies with them. Replicating the monstrous faces of gargoyles that looked down from the gothic churches of medieval Europe, they carved mythical beings such as the Green Man, the god Neptune, and the North Wind into chairs. Just like the stone carvings that had guarded sacred spaces for centuries in Europe, these faces were meant to protect your home from evil spirits—in the case of the North Wind, symbolically blowing them away.

My mother found our North Wind in a thrift store in Milwaukee for $20. As a child, I used to lie on the floor and just stare up at the face for what felt like hours. Even through my mother's mid-nineties Southwestern makeover, the dark, formidable face of the North Wind chair remained in place. It is actually quite ugly, but it is also very special.

When I moved away for school, my mother showed up just as we were finishing packing the moving truck. "I can't let you go without the chair. I want you to be protected while you're far away," she told me. To this day, it occupies a central place in my home. Among my vintage, mid-century, modern, and contemporary furniture, it sticks out like a sore thumb, but I wouldn't have it any other way.

The idea of wanting to protect your home from harmful forces, magical or otherwise, has been around for millennia. Being from the American Midwest, and of German descent, I relate easily to the idea of the North Wind being a guardian spirit of my home. Which is not to say you can't too, but I would urge you to look into your own ancestral traditions to see if they resonate with you. Again, YOU are the magic behind any spell, so the more deeply you resonate with an idea, the stronger your intentions will be.

The purpose of this chapter is to help you create an energetic force field in and around your home to protect it from negative energy.

NEGATIVE ENERGY CAN MANIFEST
IN BAD VIBES THAT JUST MAKE
IT FEEL A LITTLE OFF, OR IT
COULD COME IN THE FORM OF AN
INTRUDER——HUMAN OR SPIRIT.

Now, obviously, nothing I'm telling you here should be a substitute for taking reasonable, practical precautions like locking doors and using an added security system if necessary. But by grounding your home in positive energy and then creating a boundary of protection around it, your home will very likely feel even safer and more stable.

GROUNDING MEDITATION

A grounding meditation is a great introduction to working with psychic space, and is a crucial exercise for feeling safe and supported. It is very simple to do, yet I think you'll be amazed at how effective it can be at helping you feel centered and balanced in all areas of your life. Grounding works by creating a connection between our physical body and the center of the earth.

1

Sit in a chair with your back straight, your feet flat on the ground, and your hands on your thighs, face down. Close your eyes. Breathe deeply but calmly.

2

Imagine a green sphere of light spinning at the base of your spine. Take a few smooth, deep breaths to connect with it.

3

Picture that ball of light dropping through your body, through the chair, down through the ground all the way to the earth's core. As it drops, imagine it's leaving a green cord behind it, connecting you to the center of the planet.

4

Feel the connection between the base of your spine and the
earth. You can begin to imagine the nourishing energy of
the earth running back up your grounding cord, securing
the connection. Feel free to bring that energy all the way up
into your solar plexus energy, from where it can flow freely
throughout your body.

5

Send any negative, anxious, or unwanted energy
down your grounding cord, where the core of the earth
can recycle it into positive energy.

6

When you are ready, open your eyes, stand up,
and stretch.

It's that simple, and it is very effective. With just a little
practice, you'll soon become so comfortable grounding
yourself that you can do it with ease, wherever you
are. I used to ground every morning on the subway on the
way to work to ensure I could perform my duties from a
grounded, centered space. I believe we're all at our best
when we're able to connect easily with the earth.

OWNING A ROOM

A grounding meditation is an exercise that can stand alone in terms of its usefulness and value in your daily life, especially when working with magic. If you want to expand your psychic meditation skills, you can try "owning a room." Now, this technique does not mean that you take over a space with your energy. That would be intrusive to anyone else who lives in or spends any time in that space. What you are doing when you "own" a room is inviting your own unique frequency to expand to its full potential in that space, without compromising or competing with anyone else's ability to do the same.

1

Start by establishing or reconnecting to your grounding
cord through the grounding meditation (see page 110).

2

Bring your awareness right into the center of your head.
Imagine a space behind your third eye. Breathe deeply
until the energy in the center of your head feels calm and
clear. Having your awareness in the center of your head
should help you to stay clear and in the present moment.
Focus on staying neutral and not judging yourself for
whatever thoughts and feelings may come in. Just keep
returning to the calm feeling at the center of your head.

3

Imagine a thin green line coming from both of your feet
and reaching to the four corners of the room. These
lines represent your personal frequency. In your head say
to yourself, "My floor."

4

Imagine a thin gold line coming from the center of
your head to each corner of the ceiling. In your head,
say to yourself, "My ceiling."

5

In your head, say to yourself, "My room."

6

Send any negative, anxious or unwanted energy down your
grounding cord, to where the core of the earth
can recycle it into positive energy. When you are ready,
open your eyes, stand up, and stretch.

Grounding and owning a room can transform your relationship with the world around you. Imagine using these techniques to feel safe at home and also out in the world. These techniques can be enormously helpful in many situations that might make you nervous, or throw you off your game—think of job interviews, public speaking, or just leaving your comfort zone in general. (If you'd like to learn more about psychic meditation techniques, take a look at *Basic Psychic Development* by John Friedlander and Gloria Hemsher; for details, see Recommended Reading on page 240.)

CLAIMING SPACE

One of the simplest and most effective ways to protect your home from unseen forces (such as ghosts, spirits, or whatever you want to call them) or negative energy is by simply claiming your space as your own—stating, out loud, that this space is your space and nothing can encroach upon it without your permission. This can be done when clearing a space, or it can stand alone in moments where you feel something trespassing in your space. There are a few different ways you can approach this.

THE FRIENDLY HOUSEGUEST: you feel there is an otherworldly presence in your space, but you don't mind. Think Casper the Friendly Ghost. In this case, I would say something like, "This space is mine, and I'm the boss here. I acknowledge and respect your presence here. You're welcome to stay as long as you do no harm to the space or anyone in it." Get specific. You can set boundaries and give

Casper house rules. For example, allow free rein over one part of the space, but limit them from others. Or tell them to leave your children or pets alone. You should be gentle, but firm. Repeat your mantra in each part of your home.

THE UNWELCOME INTRUDER: you feel there is an other-worldly presence and you do mind. Think *Ghostbusters*. Here I would say, "This space is mine, and I am the boss here. I acknowledge and respect your presence here, but you are no longer welcome to stay." Follow up with some of the tools I will discuss shortly (see pages 117 to 128).

SHOWING THEM THE DOOR: as an ultimatum for ghosts behaving badly, try giving them somewhere else to go. Start by choosing something personal from the space (which you don't mind donating to the cause) and placing it outside the home. A vessel such as an old coffee mug or plant pot would work perfectly. Invite them to leave and give them an exit plan. Say something like, "This space is mine, and I am the boss here. I acknowledge and respect the time you have spent here, but that time is now over and I must ask you to leave. Please use the living room window and find the space I have created for you outside my home. Go in peace."

The most important thing is that you feel authoritative and justified in claiming your space. I would suggest doing a grounding meditation before and after these exercises so that you can feel completely balanced and centered.

USING PALO SANTO

Part of South American indigenous traditions, the name
"Palo Santo" translates as "holy wood." It comes
from the *Bursera graveolens* tree and was used by the Inca
civilization to clear negative energy from a person's
aura, while adding a bit of positivity in its wake. Its smell,
a bit like fennel or licorice, reflects the sweetness
it's adding back in. It matches the clearing power of sage,
while adding positive vibrations back into the space it's
just cleared. It comes in stick form, usually just a few inches
long, which can lend itself to being used as a writing
tool in the air, allowing you to "write" words or protective
runes in smoke all around your space.

THE PROTECTIVE POWER OF SALT

Salt can be a powerful tool for creating a safe boundary around your home. I like to work with sea salt, but if you feel connected to table salt, that works well too. When working with salt, it's good to charge it to your intention. Simply fill a bowl, or other vessel with which you feel connected, with salt and imagine a white light of positivity flowing into it from above. (You can charge your crystals in the salt at the same time.)

You can use a mortar and pestle to create a fine powder from coarse salt for use indoors, but in general I like to use salt to create a boundary around the exterior of a home. Either way, simply take your charged salt and sprinkle it in a circle around the room or around the outside of the home. If you live in an apartment, you should try to create the circle around the entire building, but feel free to leave a sprinkle outside the entrance(s) to your space as well.

Black salt is salt mixed with charcoal. You can buy it premixed or make it yourself by mixing a food-grade charcoal with salt in a mortar and pestle. Black salt is particularly good for using indoors because you'll always want to sweep it up: sprinkle the black salt around the room and sweep toward the door to remove any stuck negative energy, or use it after a person with toxic energy leaves the space.

CRYSTALS FOR PROTECTION

My go-to crystals for creating a protective boundary around both myself and my space are black tourmaline, obsidian, and amethyst. The first two are good for connecting with the center of the earth, creating a feeling of safety and security while also protecting your auric field. Amethyst connects to your highest and best mind, helping you to own your space. Here's a little more about each one.

BLACK TOURMALINE

A powerful healer and protector. Specifically used for blocking psychic attacks and unhelpful thought patterns, it grounds negative energy and leaves neutrality in its place. (Because of this, it is even said to protect against harmful electromagnetic waves caused by modern electronics such as cell phones and computers.) I carry a piece of black tourmaline in my pocket any time I'm going into a situation that makes me scared or nervous.

OBSIDIAN

Also known as volcanic glass, obsidian is made from molten lava that cooled very quickly. By nature, it works fast as a protective shield from negativity. It soaks up bad vibes like a sponge and should therefore be cleansed often. An awesome ceremony for setting an intention for protection could take the form of cleansing your obsidian under running water and visualizing all that negative energy going down the drain and out of your space. Obsidian is a great truth-teller, so it can help you get to the bottom of what's bringing negativity into your home.

AMETHYST

Mystics in the medieval ages used amethyst to treat everything from spider bites to acne. This purple sparkler is widely known and easily available in many different forms. Known for emotional and spiritual protection, amethyst can break anxious or addictive thought patterns and help you move into your higher consciousness. Its high vibration blocks negative, stressful energies and stimulates serenity of the mind. Placing an amethyst on your nightstand or under your pillow will protect you from nightmares.

Black tourmaline   *Obsidian*

Amethyst

BAD VIBES GET OUT AND STAY OUT
WINDOW AND DOOR POTION

It's best to make this potion on or near a full moon, so that you can charge it in the moonlight.

INGREDIENTS

13 drops obsidian essence

13 drops black tourmaline essence

13 drops selenite essence

13 drops essential oil, such as lavender or cedarwood

witch hazel

Add all essences and oils to a small glass bottle of your choosing. Fill the rest of the way with witch hazel. (Witch hazel acts as a preservative. You can also use vodka.) Shake to mix.

Charge under the full moon for at least one hour.

Check in with your body and the space. Do you feel centered and supported? If not, do a grounding meditation (see page 110) and try owning your space.

Once you feel like the energy in the space is yours, use a cotton ball or clean cloth to apply the potion to the frames around all of your doors and windows.

Visualize a strong protective seal forming. Feel free to call in any personal guardian angels or protective allies. (Personally, I use the archangel Michael and the animal spirits of the panther and raven.)

Ask that they create a safe boundary and stand guard around the outside of your home.

HERBAL BUNDLES

My dear friend Lauren Hall is a witch of many talents such as Reiki energy work and tarot reading, and she is also an accomplished herbalist. She uses these talents to help people clear their spaces of unwanted energies, supernatural or otherwise, through her business, Spirits and Sawdust. Her focus is on practical magic for living with ghosts, and here she teaches us—in her own words—how to make an herbal bundle for home protection:

Plant-based magic is naturally protective. Whether burning frankincense in a brazier, planting rosemary by a garden gate, or storing heirlooms in a cedar chest, we intuitively reach for it when we need to hold space.

I bring dozens of herbs to every space clearing I perform, and often craft an herbal bundle to leave behind with the home or business owner. Herbal bundles are fantastically multifunctional, serving as talismans, spells, shields, and tangible reminders of our own power.

HERBAL BUNDLE
FOR PROTECTION

INGREDIENTS

protective herbs aligned to your purpose (choose from the list to the right, or channel your own)

a mortar and pestle to mix your potion

essential oils to bring additional herbal power (and delicious scent) to your bundle

a bit of fabric that represents your specific intention (for example, black and white are strong colors for protection, yellow amplifies courage and confidence, and blue brings peace and calm)

a small item such as a crystal, coin, or keepsake connected with your goals

twine or ribbon to secure your bundle

Herbal allies for protection:

CEDAR: all trees are protective, but cedar is one of the strongest. Not only does it keep your heirlooms moth-free, it blocks all sorts of unwelcome energy from entering your space.

LAVENDER: well known for its peaceful powers, lavender is also a protective ally, bringing with it a deep well of calm, along with firm boundaries.

MUGWORT: imagine a fierce grandmother protecting her tribe through the power of her ancestors. That's mugwort.

SAGE: one of the most popular magical herbs, sage does double duty by cleansing and protecting your home at the same time.

ST. JOHN'S WORT: I often recommend St. John's wort to paranormal investigators entering spaces that feel particularly unfriendly; it's like carrying a torch into a dark place.

To create your bundle:

Gather your supplies in a quiet space in which to work. (A tabletop or counter would be helpful.) Connect with each herb, honoring its unique protective energies. When you feel ready, begin to add them, one at time, into your mortar. I typically start with a small pinch of each, but you may wish to add more of some herbs and less of others.

Next, add your essential oils, using your intuition to determine the dosage. With your pestle, grind your potion—clockwise if you're inviting in a specific intention or energy, or counterclockwise if you're banishing or clearing.

Once the mixture feels well blended, transfer it to the center of your fabric and add any small items you wish to include. Gather the edges and twist into a tight bundle, tying it off with your twine or ribbon.

Your herbal bundle is now ready for use! Place it above a door, under your bed, or any place in your space that feels particularly resonant. Once its work is complete (anywhere from a few days to a year or more), untie it and release the herbs back to the earth, with gratitude.

By now you should be feeling safe and at ease in your home, which will help you to relax and enjoy it. Next, we'll go over some ways to maximize those feelings of comfort and turn your home into a cozy retreat.

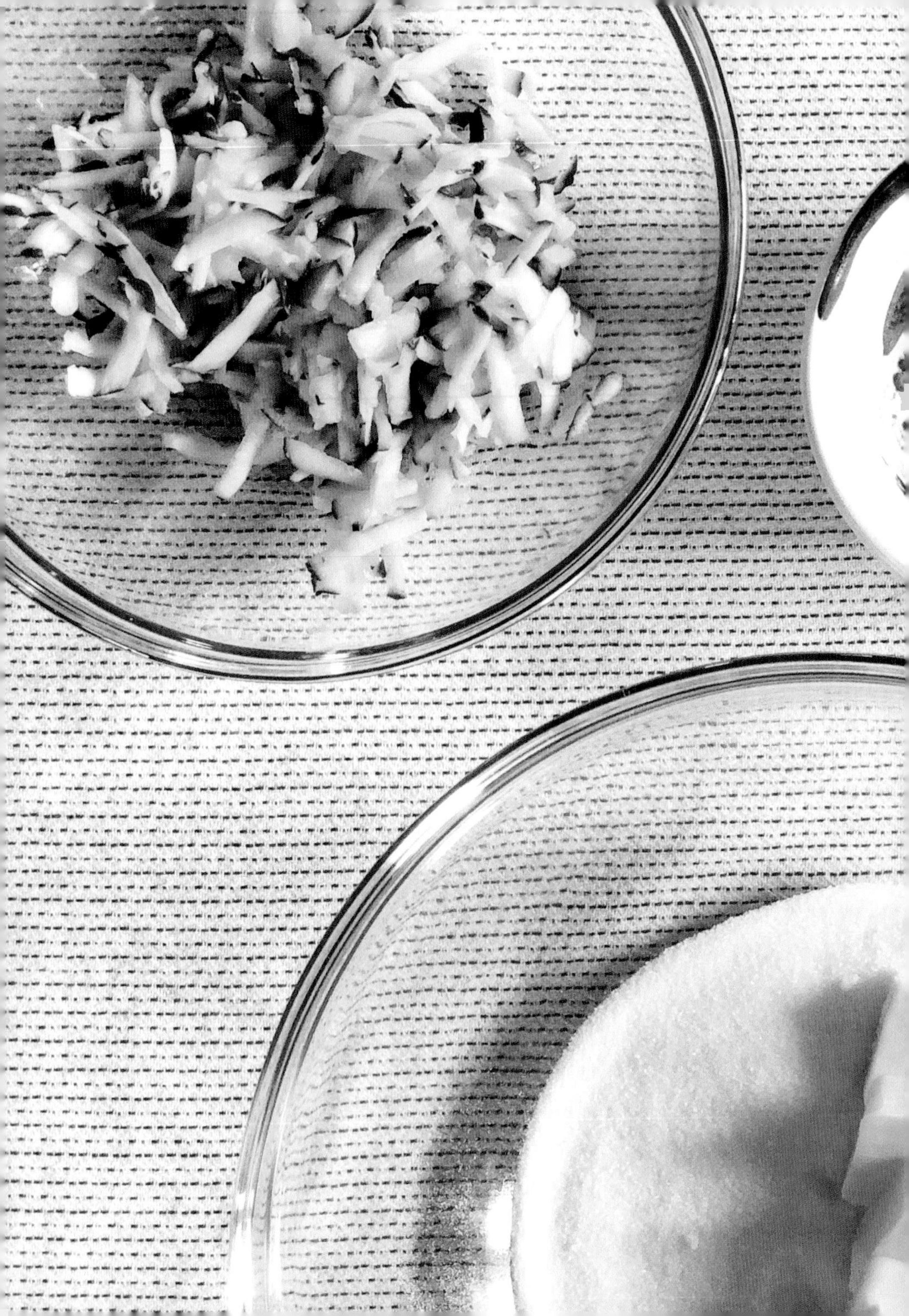

CHAPTER 4

COMFORT

I was recently forced to meditate on comfort and the purpose that it serves. Two days before Christmas, a back injury forced me to cancel my annual pilgrimage "home" to see my grandmother for the holiday. Having moved away from where I grew up, home for me became both the place where I physically lived and then a more abstract concept: a place where my family lived, where my ancestors were born and raised, the place that I came from. I had never missed a Christmas with my grandmother before and here I was, laid up, in pain, and alone.

Unconsciously, I started curating my day around feeling cozy, warm, and comfortable—big blankets, scented candles, mugs full of warm beverages. It all got a bit cliché, but it had me thinking about the spiritual function of comfort in one's personal space.

WHAT DOES FEELING "AT HOME" REALLY MEAN? HOW DO WE CULTIVATE THAT FEELING? HOW DOES IT HELP US IN OUR DAILY LIVES?

All I could control was my immediate environment and my state of mind. It made me realize that the magic of comfort isn't just about blankets and tea (although drinking tea under a blanket is a pretty good start); it's about creating an environment in which to be totally present and engaged with all six senses—taste, touch, scent, hearing, sight, and intuition—in order for your home to embody feelings of warmth and contentment in equal parts, with a pinch of nostalgia thrown in for good measure. Like a scent that makes you cock your head to the side and say, "Why is that smell so familiar?" Comfort is a spell for the senses.

I believe there are many magical and practical ways to make your home a cozier, more welcoming place. And I can tell you which things I turn to when I want to feel more comfortable and supported. But I encourage you to dive deeper into what comfort means to you. Maybe it's calling in the energy of your childhood home, or maybe you will always be chasing that feeling of listening to a certain album on an autumn day, and the way the air smelled outside.

Taste

On Christmas Eve, it turned out that baking a pan of Wisconsin-style cheesy potatoes, like my grandmother makes, was just as magical as casting a spell. I ate them while sitting wrapped in a giant blanket by the light of my fake fireplace, and I knew that everything was in alignment. By making myself physically comfortable in every way possible, it was easy to stay completely present, feel all the feels, process my emotions, and move on. I shifted from feeling like a victim of circumstance to having so much gratitude for the surprise gift of a restful, travel-free holiday.

For me, cooking is an extremely nourishing and meditative experience. A few years ago, I was away from home for several weeks, training for a new job. Having to eat in restaurants every night made me feel more homesick than anything else. I missed the simple act of chopping up garlic and throwing it in a pan with a heartache I didn't expect. Cooking might not be everyone's thing, but the kitchen is the heart of the home and engaging with it can really help to connect you with that sense of comfort. Chances are, you've got recipes that have been passed down through your family like heirlooms, and making them yourself could fill you up in the same way my grandmother's potatoes saved my Christmas.

AUTUMN EQUINOX
ROOT VEGETABLE STEW

This lovely stew is perfect for easing into the colder months. Hearty without being heavy, a colorful variety of root vegetables and fresh thyme is perfect for invoking some seriously autumnal vibes. Plus, thyme has been used for centuries to bring inner courage and strength to the person using it. Its aroma can help rid your home of melancholy and despair.

INGREDIENTS

1.5 L (2½ pts.) of turkey or vegetable broth

1 medium sweet potato (peeled and chopped)

1 medium turnip (peeled and chopped)

1 medium parsnip (peeled and chopped)

2 carrots (chopped)

1 small yellow onion (chopped)

1 tablespoon fresh thyme

1 teaspoon salt

freshly ground pepper, to taste

300 g (11 oz.) cooked turkey (if preferred, substitute this with cannellini beans or a meat substitute)

chopped parsley, for topping

In a large cauldron/soup pot, combine all of your ingredients, except for the turkey and parsley. Bring your concoction to a boil.

Cover your stew, reduce heat to medium-low, and simmer for fifteen to twenty minutes.

Add the turkey (or your substitute) and simmer, uncovered, for about ten more minutes.

Ladle into big bowls, and sprinkle a little parsley over the top.

FULL MOON CHOCOLATE ZUCCHINI CAKE

My mom used to make this chocolate cake to trick us into eating some vegetables. The zucchini makes the cake super moist but doesn't affect the overall chocolaty goodness. Cocoa is a rich source of antioxidants, which can help heal your skin and are said to reduce stress (yes please!). Magically, it will also help you connect to your heart in a way that allows for deep healing. For an added lunar boost, charge the cocoa powder under the full moon for half an hour before using. To do this, simply measure out the powder and put it in a beautiful bowl, dish, or cup and leave on a windowsill in the moonlight.

INGREDIENTS

100 g (3½ oz.) white sugar

65 g (2¼ oz.) brown sugar

100 g (3½ oz.) butter

2 tablespoons vegetable oil

½ teaspoon vanilla extract

2 eggs

200 g (7 oz.) flour

15 g (½ oz.) moon-charged unsweetened cocoa powder

½ teaspoon baking soda

¼ teaspoon ground cinnamon

60 mL (3 tablespoons) buttermilk (or mix ¼ teaspoon lemon juice or vinegar with milk and leave to stand for 5 minutes before using)

150 g (5 oz.) shredded zucchini

75 g (3 oz.) (or more to taste) plain chocolate chips

25 cm (10 in.) round cake tin (greased)

moon-phase stencil

confectioners' sugar (for dusting)

HAUSMAGICK

Preheat your oven to 160°C (325°F).

In large bowl, combine the white and brown sugars, butter, oil, vanilla, and eggs. Beat well. Next, add the flour, cocoa, baking soda, cinnamon, and buttermilk, blending well with an electric mixer.

Now add the shredded zucchini and chocolate chips, mixing well by hand. Spread the mixture in the greased pan, and bake in the preheated oven for 30–40 minutes or until a toothpick comes out clean when poked into the mixture. Cool completely.

To make the stencil, trace shapes (see photo) onto parchment paper and carefully cut these out with scissors or a craft knife. Lay on top of the cooled cake and sprinkle confectioners' sugar on top.

Touch

When I think of cozy, I think of the sweaters and flannel blankets that come out in the autumn and winter months, but "soft" is just one texture that evokes comfort. To convey a sense of warmth and coziness, I suggest having many different layers of texture in your space. This will help it to feel more lived in, dynamic, and ultimately comforting.

Glass, ceramics, and mirrors are smooth materials that bring in calm, relaxing energy. Windows, mirrors, and glass objects have the added practical benefit of bouncing light around to cast more natural light into dark spaces. A beautiful glass or ceramic vessel filled with water and flowers adds visual interest with its curved lines, while symbolizing emotional control in the way that a vessel contains water.

Decor that brings in natural textures associated with trees, plants, and growth—such as hardwood floors, wood furniture and cabinets, cotton blankets or curtains, and rugs—provides a grounding connection to the earth. Aside from the tactile feel of these items, they also provide an opportunity to bring in design elements such as woodgrain, patterned fabric, and knits.

Finally, items that physically provide warmth are important in establishing comfort in a space. Literally and metaphorically, warmth is almost synonymous with feelings of coziness. A crackling fireplace is the ideal example of a warming tactile element, but candles are great as well. I have a space heater made to look like a fireplace, and it does the job quite nicely!

Scent

One of the most common ways to feel nurtured in your space is by using smells to capture a particular feeling or sense of nostalgia. Studies have shown that feelings of nostalgia actually make the body feel physically warmer and more supported. This is because scent has the ability to tap into our collective memory and help us recall nourishing memories of family, nature, seasonal changes, and good times. (A hero of mine, Dr. Carl Gustav Jung, worked extensively with the idea of a "collective unconscious," which is based on the notion that there is a realm of universal ideas and archetypes that we can all tap into.)

Scent can be very powerful in spell work because of its ability to transport you to a different time and place. Closing your eyes and inhaling a scent that has a powerful association for you can create an alternate reality of sorts, taking you out of the mundane world and into a more spiritual realm. I always include an aromatherapy element in my spell work, and for this reason I prefer to use scented candles (as opposed to colored or shaped ones) and incense to help set my intentions.

Just like burning sage and other herbs has an effect on the energetic vibration of a space, so does incense smoke. My favorite incense for calling in warmth and abundance is cinnamon. Cinnamon is a spice that runs at a high vibration and improves energy flow. It is also associated with abundance, and what's a more supportive feeling than enjoying a sense of plenty? Nag Champa is another incense that is nostalgic for many people as it is burned for a wide variety of reasons. But my number one most nostalgic smell is that of burning wood in the autumn and winter. To re-create this, I use high-quality, hand-rolled copal and resin incense sticks.

Candles and incense aren't the only way to bring in good smells. With just a few essential oils, you can make a potent potion to gently scent your space. Play around with blends that make you say "mmm." Everyone reacts to scent differently, but most people associate warm, woodsy, or food-based smells with comfort. Try playing around with pine, fir, clove, cassia, vanilla, and orange to invoke comfort and familiarity.

HAUSWARMING POTION

INGREDIENTS

15 drops orange essential oil

15 drops cassia essential oil

15 drops cedarwood essential oil

For a quick sensory journey, just add a blend of essential oils to a ceramic bowl or mug. Then add boiling water and—BOOM!—you're in cozy town. The steam will float the scent throughout your space.

In love with that smell? Turn this potion into a room spray by adding the oil blend to a 60 mL/2 fl. oz. spray bottle and fill the rest of the way with equal parts water and witch hazel. (Witch hazel acts as a preservative. You can also use vodka.) For an extra boost, make a citrine essence and add a few drops of that (see "How to Create a Crystal Essence Potion," page 42).

Hearing

There are a few ways to use sound to set a mood for your space. Sound healing works as vibrational medicine, just like crystals do. You can infuse a particular sound-healing vibration into a space (see page 94) by clearing it with whatever method you choose (smoke, bells, clapping, etc.) and then playing soothing music to fill the space back up. A friend of mine uses Mozart to inspire creativity.

To infuse your space with a meditative vibe, try some New Age music or a white noise frequency to focus. (As I write, I am listening to theta brain wave–inducing binaural beats on YouTube, which allows me to concentrate. This particular frequency helps distract the overactive part of my brain so that I am able to work.)

Complete silence is hard to find, but try turning off all of your electronics to achieve some level of stillness. Total silence can be extremely calming and can help you hear messages from your guides more clearly. On the other end of the spectrum: experiment with soundscapes! The magic of the internet affords us access to many different audio options for making our space feel like home.

Placing bells on your door or chimes outside your window can create little audible reminders of home. The wind then becomes a part of your space and helps you feel connected to the earth even if you're in a more urban area.

Sight

Lighting is hugely important for creating a comfortable, cozy space. Conventional wisdom says each room should have three different light sources. Now, this next bit is very important, so, please, if you take nothing else from this book for your home, do this:

BUY MORE LAMPS AND . . .
TURN OFF THE OVERHEAD LIGHT
IN YOUR ROOM FOREVER!

Changing their lighting has made the single biggest difference out of anything I've done for most of my clients. Overhead lighting is cold, impersonal, and unflattering for every human, animal, and object. By adding lamps, you can control how much or how little light an area of a room gets, completely changing the vibe and the mood. You can even play around with the light bulb wattages (which I do obsessively and would suggest you at least try), or buy bulbs with multiple levels of brightness built in. A table lamp here and a floor lamp there will dramatically improve the look and feel of any room instantly. This is the HausWitch #1 gold-star, blue-ribbon tip that I can offer you.

Of course, the most magical light of all is natural light. Nothing makes people stop in their tracks quite like a room with beautiful natural light. It honestly hurts my heart when I walk into a room where the curtains or blinds are always drawn. Studies in many different fields, from architecture to medicine, have shown that the natural light and air offered by windows help people to feel better and actually heal faster from illness or injury. If privacy is an issue, I suggest buying curtains that are sheer enough to let some natural light still filter through them.

Intuition

Intuition is our sixth sense, as essential in magical and divinatory practices as any of the other five. It's key to creating a living space that feels balanced and harmonious, and that makes you feel truly—intuitively—"at home."

CRYSTALS FOR COMFORT

In the context of comfort, crystals are the perfect way to connect supportive earth energy to our sixth sense of intuition. The crystals I rely on to hold a warm, soothing, positive vibration in my home are carnelian, citrine, and tree agate.

CARNELIAN

A wise young witch once told me I could use carnelian as a candle substitute in spell work, because there is so much fire in this reddish-orange beauty. Which is precisely why I like it for warming up a space energetically. With its swirls of red, orange, and brown, carnelian can wake you up like a spark, yet keep you feeling grounded and safe at the same time. It's going to help you feel comfortable without being lazy or complacent.

CITRINE

My go-to rock for good vibes in general. A yellowish-orange type of quartz, citrine sparks creativity and increases your ability to welcome abundance into your life. Like a ray of sunshine, citrine is like a crystal cheerleader, reminding you that you have everything you need. Mix citrine essence in a potion with orange, clove, and cinnamon essential oils to make a room spray that will feel like a sunbeam (see page 42, on making crystal essences, for tips on how to do this).

TREE AGATE

To balance all that fire and sunshine, throw tree agate into the mix. The key words with this swirly green stone are "grounding" and "stabilizing." It's like kicking off your shoes so as to feel rooted to the earth under your feet, helping you to feel completely supported. For this reason, this one is great for using in an all-natural floor wash too.

Carnelian

Citrine

Tree agate

COZY FROM THE GROUND UP
FLOOR WASH

INGREDIENTS

10 drops fir essential oil

10 drops juniper berry essential oil

5 drops orange essential oil

13 drops tree agate essence

85 g (3 oz.) Sals Suds (or Castile soap)

30 mL (1 fl. oz.) vodka (a preservative and disinfectant)

1 bucket of warm water

Mix together the ingredients in the bucket of warm water and clean your floors with this mixture on a Sunday, when the moon is in an earth sign (i.e., Virgo, Capricorn, or Taurus). Sunday is ruled by the sun, ruler of strength and light. When combined with the tree agate's stability and grounding, these energies will create a perfect balance of calm and contentment. Plus, your space will smell like a sweet walk through the woods in the winter.

The scent of orange can lift the spirits and elevate your mood, whereas juniper calms the nervous system, helping to reduce anxiety, and fir can make you feel more confident.

HESTIA HEARTH WALL HANGING

MATERIALS

1 naturally sourced branch of wood

hemp or leather cord for hanging the branch

at least 6 meters of organic cotton cord

1 piece of raw carnelian

selection of wooden beads, feathers, and/or other red and orange crystals (optional)

essential oil spray, such as the HausWarming potion, see page 151 (optional)

Hestia was the Greek goddess of home and hearth (or Vesta, in Roman mythology). She is known for the eternal flame that burned in temples devoted to her. Invoking her in your space will bring warmth and wellness. In order to bring her in, we need to open your home's heart, through its hearth.

Don't have a fireplace? No worries, we can make one. My dear friend Jessica Jones Lavoie of Evolving Light Energy is going to show us how. Jessica is an energy healer who mainly works with Reiki and essential oils. Her wall hangings, which she calls Wall Spells, are made with natural elements such as wood, cotton, crystals, and feathers, and they look fantastic in any room. We came up with this idea as a way to add a visual and energetic fireplace to any space that doesn't already have one.

1. CONNECT

When creating a wall hanging (or "Wall Spell") that
is going to feel like the heart of your space, the first step is
to connect with how that heart feels to you. Visualize
your home and hearth exactly where she wants to be—write
down any words or images that come through. These
feelings, scenes, colors, etc. will help shape your personal
intentions for your hearth, what it'll look like, and where
it'll live in your space.

2. GATHER

Let the foraging begin! Use your notes from step 1 and
a little research to explore which ingredients would support
your vision—and don't be surprised when you're gifted
the stone you're looking for, or stumble on the perfect tree
limb. We want to bring in warmth, vitality, and fire,
so we will also be using raw carnelian (see page 156).

3. CREATE

Once you have sourced your materials, start with your
wood base and create a hanger for it using some
hemp or leather cord. Cut eight pieces of your cotton cord
at roughly equal lengths, at least 60 cm/24 in. long.

4. DISPLAY

Time to let your wall spell shine and energetically warm
up your space. If you don't already have a spot in
mind, try meditating to discover the perfect place for
your new Hestia Hearth.

Attach each piece of cord to your driftwood base (or whatever you're using) by folding the strand in half and putting the loop head over the driftwood, then pulling the rest of the fiber through the loop. Pull down on each doubled strand to tighten. Do this until all your fiber strands are attached to your wall-hanging base.

Now you can decide what you want to add. You can simply tie your carnelian and other crystals straight on to your hanging strands, or add beads, ethically sourced feathers, and more crystals. The more of your energy and creativity that you add, the more your fireplace will be charged with your good vibes. If you want to get fancy, try adding some macramé or woven elements!

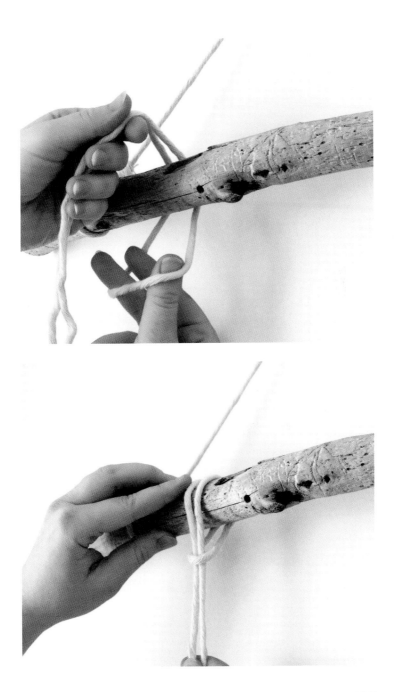

Never underestimate the power of cozy! Your ability to establish feelings of comfort in your home will be reflected in how rested and recharged you feel when you leave it. Next up, we'll look at how to create harmony in a home that you share with others.

crafted home

Explode Every Day

An Inquiry into the Phenomena of Wonder

EVERY
DAY
COUNTS

FANTASTISK

CHAPTER 5

HARMONY

YOUR HOME SHOULD BE YOUR SANCTUARY, WHERE YOU CAN BE AT YOUR FREEST AND LEAST SELF-CONSCIOUS.

You need a place where you can relax and take up space, your own little corner of the world. But living in harmony with others, whether they be friends, lovers, roommates, or pets, isn't always easy. When the same space fills emotional needs for more than one person, things can get complicated.

We know the importance of sharing, compromise, and coming together, but setting boundaries to separate our energy from that of others is just as important. Those boundaries are what make it possible for us to live in healthy relationships with other people and connect with them on deeper and more authentic levels. The ability to mind your energy will ultimately bring you even closer to the people nearest to you.

Boundaries

Everyone has an auric field, more commonly known as an aura. Your aura is your personal electromagnetic field and it extends two to three feet around the outside of your body. The wavelength and color of your aura changes depending on your surroundings, who you're with, your emotional state, and many other things. Your aura can pick up other energies that don't necessarily belong to you. It is your job to keep your aura clear of outside influences.

One of the most important parts of living a magically empowered life is knowing how to distinguish between your energy and the energy of others.

EVEN POSITIVE ENERGY CAN STIFLE YOUR OWN, IF IT DOES NOT BELONG TO YOU.

The good news is that you are always in control of your energy, and no one can force their energy onto you without your conscious (or unconscious) agreement. You can always take your energy back from others and return theirs to them as well. When living with others it is a good idea to do this from time to time through visualization techniques.

SIMPLE VISUALIZATION
FOR ENERGY AWARENESS

Doing this exercise periodically will shift the relationships
you have with other people, and you'll find
you have greater control over your emotions. Once you
have a better sense of your personal energy field,
you will be able to set effective boundaries around it.

1

Start with the Grounding Meditation and Owning a Room
exercise as outlined on pages 110–13. These exercises are
foundational to building an awareness of
your energy and the energy of others.

2

Now visualize your aura. It's okay if you have a hard time
with this at first. Just imagine a glowing light around
your body. If it shows up as a color, fantastic! If there
is no color, that's okay too. The point is simply to be able
to see your energy field in your mind's eye.

3

Think of a person with whom you have interacted recently.
The interaction could be good, bad, or indifferent. You
should try to keep your emotions as neutral as possible.

See if you can pick up on any changes in your visualization
of your aura when you think of that person. Does it show
up as a different color? A dark spot? A bright light? Does it
affect the overall energy of your aura or just a part?

4

Try to visualize that person's energy leaving your aura and
going back to theirs. Use any visuals that resonate with you.
Maybe the energy looks like smoke, or water, or a beam
of light. Get as creative as you'd like, as long as you can
sense the other person's energy leaving your auric field.

5

Now do the reverse. Imagine your energy coming back
to you from them. Send any energy that doesn't feel
like it's serving your best intentions down your grounding
cord and into the center of the earth.

6

Finish by imagining a golden light around yourself,
filling in any holes that the other person's energy may have
left behind.

HEALTHY BOUNDARIES BATH

Feel like your energetic boundaries could use some strengthening? On a Saturday (ruled by Saturn, the planet of structure and limits), make this tub tea to help you relax and to support your boundaries.

INGREDIENTS

a pinch of dried rose for soothing, protective, heart-healing energy

a pinch of dried yarrow for boundaries and balance

a pinch of dried rosemary for protection and confidence

a pinch of salt (sea, Epsom, or pink Himalayan)

rose or lavender essential oil, known to aid relaxation

1 small muslin pouch

Combine equal parts of the herbs and salt in a bowl. Mix in a few drops of essential oil. Put the mixture into the muslin pouch. While filling the bath tub, hang the pouch on the tap like a teabag so that the hot water runs through it into the tub. Soak.

Combining Decorating Styles

Now you've set your energetic boundaries, let's look at the decor choices that can also enhance harmonious living.

It's important to make sure that everyone living under the same roof is able to have their voice heard, their boundaries respected, and their tastes represented. No matter how different you and your housemate's aesthetic preferences are, there is a way to mesh them, I promise.

When a space feels and looks better in general as a result of small changes, even the most stubborn tastes can be shifted for the greater good—and a little good intention is the most tasteful thing you can add to any room.

TIPS FOR SUCCESSFUL STYLE ALCHEMY

MINIMALIST/MAXIMALIST: one of you likes the space sparse and one likes it busy. Why not try to keep trinkets and bric-a-brac to a minimum, but allow for some eclectic curation? Or layers of colorful pillows or a big, patterned rug in an otherwise streamlined room? Keep 80 percent of the areas clutter free, but give over 20 percent of the space to a dramatic gallery wall or an overgrown collection that is displayed tastefully. The key is to keep the decor neutral and the overall space clear, which will make a little controlled chaos go a long way.

You can also reverse this idea, letting bright, loud wallpaper or a combination of different upholstery patterns, for example, dominate across 20 percent of the visual space, but keep the rest of the space and its surfaces clear, neutral, and minimal. Always try to keep the ratio the same.

IF IT'S FLAT, FRAME IT!: maybe there is something sentimental you can frame, like a postcard from a trip you took together or a map of your hometown? Your astrological birth charts? Any memorabilia from shared experiences will create harmony and bring positive energy to the space.

PRIVATE SPACES: each person living in the space should have their own private place—a little island of one's own where you can have everything exactly how you want it. This can be a whole separate room, part of a room, or even just a shelf on a bookcase. My wife and I share an open loft space, but we've still designated little areas of our own. I have a little space in our living area for my writing desk and books. She has a work space off our kitchen, with a table for creating artwork and a cabinet for storing supplies. I have my space exactly how I want it and she has hers. Giving our individual auras the room in which to expand makes it easier to combine our tastes in the common areas of the shared space.

ART DEPICTING HAPPY COUPLES OR GROUPS: a Feng Shui method for fostering love and romance in your bedroom is to hang artwork in there that depicts happy couples or pairs (as in a pair of deer or a pair of trees, you get the point). Why not extend this idea to the whole house and your roommates as well? The important thing to remember is that the art you choose is setting an intention for your home too. Think of it as an "art spell." Choosing art where the subjects are in harmonious relationship with each other is a safe bet for a happy home.

MAKE A VENN DIAGRAM: I know, this doesn't sound very witchy or glamorous, but it can really help to identify some common ground when it comes to decorating.

Ask yourselves these questions:

Which three words (or another small number—to make the scope tighter and the challenge easy to do) describe how you want the space to feel?

Which three colors would you like to be surrounded with?

What are your favorite things about the space as it is now?

What textures and/or materials do you like?

Arrange the words and elements in a Venn diagram to clarify what your shared values are and highlight how the differences might sit together. For example:

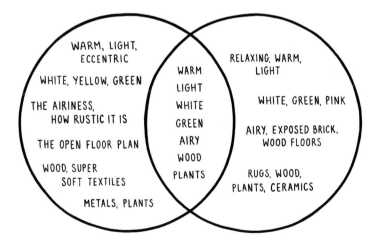

CRYSTALS FOR HARMONY

There are many stones that can connect to your heart and leave you more open to giving and receiving positive energy to and from others who share your space. Green and pink stones are great for connecting with your heart, or try something blue to open the lines of communication. Here are some of my favorites for bringing harmony home.

LEPIDOLITE

A great stone for bringing in lightness and serenity. It can connect your heart to your intuition, helping you navigate your interactions with others. It encourages strength in the face of hostility, while fostering a deeper understanding of the lessons we can learn in tough situations.

MOONSTONE

A great neutralizer, this stone promotes emotional intelligence by calming overreactions and encouraging empathy. Moonstone holds a passive feminine vibration, which can balance out aggressive Yang energy and encourage calm. Try placing a moonstone in each corner of a room to ease ongoing tension and soothe emotional triggers.

ROSE QUARTZ

This beautiful crystal connects strongly to the heart and is my go-to love spell stone. It amplifies self-love, which is the foundation for loving others and for having that love reciprocated. Rose quartz heals emotional wounds, fills your aura with good vibes, and dissolves resentments.

Lepidolite

Moonstone

Rose quartz

Pet Whispering

If you live with house pets then you know that their energy takes up just as much (if not more) of the psychic and emotional space in your home as the energy of the people who live there.

My coven's go-to animal whisperer is Madeline Mooney. Madeline grew up in the forests of Vermont and has a strong connection to nature spirits. She also has a one-eared black cat named Jasper and is amazing at psychically communicating with all our Haus pets. Here she gives us a quick meditation designed to help you to bond with your non-human roommates:

PSYCHIC PET COMMUNICATION

Conversing with your pet is simpler than you might think! We ourselves are part of the animal world, and can connect with them through a language we all share— our intuition. Every being, large or small, has the ability to communicate psychically. For humans, it simply takes learning to trust our intuitive capacity.

One way intuition works is through clairvoyance, or inner sight. Clairvoyance is used in meditation, when we see images within our minds. Clairaudience involves hearing messages within the mind. Each of these gifts stems from the third eye, the energy center located in the space between our eyebrows. During this exercise, we will use our clairvoyant and clairaudient selves to see and hear the intuitive messages our pets have to share.

1

Find a quiet spot where you can sit beside your pet. If there is a place where you typically connect, go there. Do not be discouraged if your pet moves around in the room throughout this task (or even leaves it), as you can continue to communicate intuitively, regardless of location. Another important note is not to confine your pet in any unusual way. Let them roam as they typically would, so you can both communicate with clarity and confidence.

2

Once you are settled, close your eyes and center into your breath. Sense the connection of your body to the earth, and begin to imagine yourself surrounded by crystalline white light. See yourself drawing light into your body as you inhale, and watch it surround you as you exhale.

3

Now envision your pet, wherever they are, surrounded by the same clear, white light. See their aura fill and expand just as yours did.

4

Next, imagine a beam of white light extending from your third eye to your pet's third eye.

5

When this connection is clear, you can begin to listen to, or communicate with, your pet in whatever way you feel guided to. You can speak to him or her in the same way you would speak to a human. Listen for answers to your questions within your mind. You might ask, "How can I support you?" or "What would you like to share today?" Trust in your ability to hear your pet's voice, as well your ability to send love through psychic connection.

Every animal has a message to share; all we need to do is listen! The more we open to communicating with pets, the easier it will become. Enjoy this practice as a tool for deepening your relationship with pets as friends and family members.

Tarot for Lovers, Friends, and Roommates

I turn, here, to my own roommate, romantic partner, and tarot reader, Melissa Nierman, who has offered a tarot spread designed to help you understand the dynamics at play in your home:

The tarot is a mirror. And, yes, also a deck of cards. Where most people go wrong with the tarot is believing that it can predict the future. The tarot, in fact, is a tool of reflection that only shares what you already know. So why bother with the tarot if you already know what it's going to tell you? Because what we know isn't always accessible on a conscious level. Everyday life can really distract us from hearing our inner voice and connecting to our intuition. This can be especially true in relationships, since we carry with us so many emotional wounds, past patterns, and triggers concerning them. Relationships themselves are really the best mirror around, if you can connect to what's happening underneath the mundane, everyday interactions.

When living with another person—whether a flatmate, a parent, a sibling, a husband, or a lover—any patterns or triggers you experience in your relationships will be amplified. There's no real way of hiding any of it, and if you try, all that built-up angst, anger, sadness, or annoyance is going to manifest into, say, a passive-aggressive note left on the sink about how the other person never washes the dishes; or maybe it will appear in the form of a full-blown fight that seems to come out of nowhere, and ends with doors slamming and feelings hurt.

It's not always easy to initiate those hard discussions about difficult feelings, especially if you can't completely explain why your flatmate feels like the most irritating person in the entire world, or why you dread going home. That's where the tarot comes in. It's not just a way of seeing yourself more clearly, but of seeing entire situations more clearly, and it can create the space in which to actually talk about issues openly and honestly, without awkwardness. Tarot can be the objective third party that doesn't take sides.

Your home is a co-created experience, an environment that reflects the combination of your two (or more) energies. Sometimes the combination is harmonious, as suggested by the Lovers card—a balanced merging of parts—or sometimes it's a little less comfortable, as symbolized by the Tower, which is all about letting foundations crumble if these no longer serve you. Whatever cards come up, there are various interpretations for each of them (see pages 202 to 205). Use the imagery of your deck as a source of information too, and pay attention to repeated themes between the cards, colors, numbers, and any feelings that the cards may trigger. Keep in mind that you will understand your own situation better than the best tarot guidebook ever could—although a good guidebook can be very helpful.

7 OF WANDS

10 OF

Crusader Candle Co.,Inc. Brooklyn 15, N.Y.

THE HARMONIOUS
HAUS SPREAD

There's lots of ways to pull tarot cards. A tarot spread
consists of specific questions that you want to dig deeper
into, and hopefully shed some light on. Like a good
road map, a good spread can lead you to where you want
to go as efficiently and painlessly as possible. For the
spread that will follow here, you'll use only the Major
Arcana cards. Just like your relationships and your home,
this is a co-created experience.

1

Remove the Minor Arcana cards from the deck that
you'll be using. Then gather your housemates in a shared
area of your home, such as the living room or
kitchen. Everyone should close their eyes and take three
deep breaths to arrive and be present in the space.

2

Ask each person to shuffle the cards before pulling any. It
is important to have each participant's energy in the deck.

3

Spread the cards out, face-down, in a straight
or curved line.

4

Either out loud or silently, the first person
should ask, "What energy am I bringing into
our home?" and draw a card.

5

Repeat for each person participating.

6

Lastly, everyone should concentrate on the question,
"What kind of dynamic is the combination of these energies
bringing into the home?" and choose a card together.
Maybe this means one person is designated to choose for
the group, or you establish physical contact with each other
while you choose. That part is up to you.

7

The most important thing is to support each other in
whatever comes up. Stay open, curious, and willing to use
the information as a source of positive change.

THREE-CARD
RELATIONSHIP SPREAD

This is a simple variant on the Harmonious Haus spread,
which you can use for two people. Since people are
always growing and changing you can do this spread
periodically as a way of checking in with the
energies of your home.

1

What energy is Person A currently bringing to the home?

2

What energy is Person B currently bringing to the home?

3

What kind of dynamic is the combination of these energies
currently creating in the home?

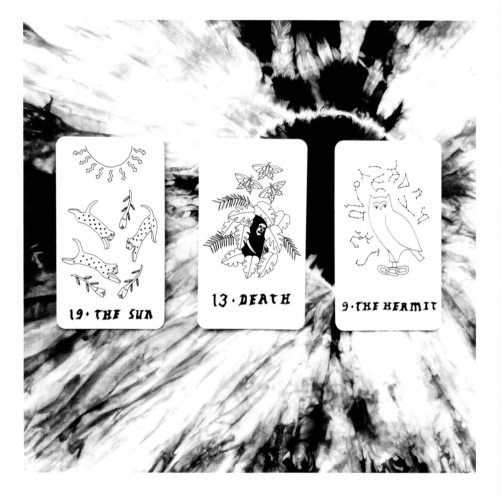

MAJOR ARCANA KEY MEANINGS

Here are some basic Major Arcana meanings to help you on your way in your relationship tarot readings. Pay close attention to any thoughts or spontaneous feelings that come up when working with these cards.

Number	Name	Key Meanings
0	THE FOOL	Beginnings, innocence, leap of faith into unknown, naïve.
1	MAGICIAN	Manifesting, alchemist, makes things happen, creative.
2	HIGH PRIESTESS	Centered, inner voice, intuitive, quiet wisdom.
3	EMPRESS	Divine feminine, abundance, loving, giving generously.
4	EMPEROR	Divine masculine, structure, authority, boundaries, takes up space.

Number	Name	Key Meanings
5	HIEROPHANT	Teacher, role model, institutions, mediator.
6	LOVERS	Merging of two parts, balance, harmony, working together.
7	CHARIOT	Ambition, expansion, drive to succeed, makes the most out of opportunities.
8	STRENGTH	Emotional control, courage, grace under pressure, calming.
9	HERMIT	Going inward, finding own truths, solitude, inner light.
10	WHEEL OF FORTUNE	Destiny, cycles of life, fate, serendipity, chance, "you never know what you're gonna get."

Number	Name	Key Meanings
11	JUSTICE	Cause and effect, making choices and living with the consequences, responsibility, fairness and equality.
12	HANGED MAN	Letting go, surrender, being stuck, transition, waiting.
13	DEATH	Death of ego, going through transformation, ending that brings new start.
14	TEMPERANCE	Bringing opposites into balance, moderation, ease and flow, healing influence.
15	DEVIL	Bondage, addiction, self-destructive tendencies, toxicity, need to let go.

Number	Name	Key Meanings
16	TOWER	Sudden change, disruption, release, letting go of that which no longer serves you.
17	STAR	Healing, newfound hope, lightness and high vibes, newfound individuality.
18	MOON	Illusive, mysterious, "lunacy," in the void or shadow realm, listening deeply.
19	SUN	Confidence, vitality, letting light shine, acceptance of self, authenticity.
20	JUDGMENT	Release of old patterns, in a place of gratitude and fulfillment, forgiveness, feeling whole.
21	WORLD	Completion, celebration, at the ending of one cycle, the beginning of another, opening to universe, YES!

Now that everyone's boundaries have been respected and their tastes acknowledged, all of the inhabitants of your space should feel at home. The last piece of the puzzle is balance, which will bring together all of your other intentions—and invite a calm serenity into your home.

CHAPTER 6

BALANCE

So here we are, at the end of this book! You've put a lot of effort into making your home a sacred space, and now it is time to bring it into balance. For me, it's important to take both energetics and aesthetics into account when creating balance in a home. Here's what I mean. . . .

A few years ago, I was having a lot of trouble decorating a room in my place. It was a two-bedroom apartment, which meant there was an extra room that my partner and I were using as an office, which doubled as a guest room when needed. However, no matter how many makeovers and tweaks I gave it, we never really wanted to spend much time in it. The rest of the apartment was a beautiful, light-filled space with lots of windows, and this room was darker and looked out onto a brick wall and the alley where our trash cans were kept. My last-ditch effort was to paint all of the furniture in the room white and yellow in an effort to brighten up the space. But again, as with all the makeovers that came before it, the space still looked and felt terrible.

About a week later, I was talking to Christopher, my clairvoyant, via Skype. I asked him if he could drop into the space intuitively and read the energy of the room. He agreed.

The first thing he said was, "The room is naturally dark, right?"

"Yep."

"Stop trying to make it light."

"Okay."

"Is the room filled with work papers and junk?"

"Yep."

"It doesn't want to be filled with work papers and junk."

"Okay."

"The room doesn't want to be a productive space. It wants to be a creative space. A meditative place. And it wants to be dark. With candles. Wait, is there like, a yellow bookcase in there?"

"Yep."

"Yeah, that's going to have to go."

And just like that, the ideas for decorating it started flowing. The room wants to be dark? Cool, a black chalkboard wall should take care of that. Creative? Great, I'm going to build an arts-and-crafts table that takes up an entire wall! Meditative? Candles? I can do that!

In the end, what my bright, sunny apartment needed was some moon energy. Some dark to balance the light. A little Yin to balance out the Yang. As someone who is naturally drawn to light, airy spaces, I never thought about the need for dark. Of course that room soon became one of our favorite spaces in the house, and guests loved staying in such a creatively charged space.

The lesson I learned was that you can throw all of the aesthetic fixes you know at a space and it can still feel imbalanced energetically. The two have to work together— aesthetics and energetics. It's about combining the material world and the astral plane.

Think about what this means to you. Take the time to get clear about what intentions you can set to feel calm and balanced in your space—and how to achieve this. Can you close your eyes and try to hear what the space wants you to know? Or are there certain activities you do at home that are making the place feel stressful rather than serene? Do you bring work home with you? Is that helping you create a sacred, restful space? Maybe there's a way to create separation in your space to accommodate a better balance? A huge shift for me came about when I stopped checking work emails from my couch. That simple change helped to keep my couch a soft island of relaxation rather than an extension of my work space. Overall, the energy in your home takes its cues from you. If your energy is in a balanced, centered place, your home will reflect that.

SUPER EASY BREATHWORK
FOR INSTANT CALM

Try this exercise when you arrive home after a
busy day. In addition to dissolving some of that frenetic
energy out of your auric field (see page 173), it will
physically calm your nervous system. It is a restorative
yoga technique that not only restores balance but which
can help alleviate acute anxiety or feelings of panic.

1

Sit in the center of your space or as close to it
as physically possible.

2

Set a timer for two minutes.

3

Take a few deeps breaths to situate yourself.

4

Do the grounding meditation (see page 110).

5

Start your timer.

6

Now change your breathing so that your exhales
are twice as long as your inhales.

7

Continue until the timer goes off.

8

Notice the space around you. The energy, even the air
itself, should feel calmer and more balanced.

Decorating for Balance

When spell-crafting, I like to use the four elements as a guide for creating balanced spells, and I do this by being sure to include something that represents each one of them. This usually takes the form of using, for example, a candle to symbolize the element of fire, incense for air, a crystal for earth, and water for, well, water. (However, an empty cup, bowl, or shell can also represent water in a similar way to how, in the tarot, the suit of cups relates to water.) I invite you to extend this idea to decorating.

Think of some decorative items and which element you think they represent. You can use properties such as colors, textures, and materials as ways to categorize your stuff. For example, I will always equate bright colors with fire, muted blues and blacks with water, neutrals like brown and gray with earth, and pastels and whites with air. Smooth textures such as glass remind me of water, whereas lamps and natural light make me think of air, and I equate textiles with earth and bold statement pieces with fire.

Once you've divided up your decor this way, take an inventory. Are you heavy on one particular element? How do you relate to that element? Maybe you are a Leo who is drawn to a lot of fiery decor? If that's the case, try working in some cooler tones or smooth textures for balance.

SYMMETRY

Another way to introduce balance in decorating is to think about symmetry. This is not to say that everything must be absolutely symmetrical, but there are some ways symmetry can be useful. One example is bedside tables. If you and your partner live together, and presumably share a bed, then your bedside tables should be symmetrical. They don't have to match perfectly, but ideally they should be similar in size and shape. If they aren't, not only will the room feel imbalanced, but the dynamics of your relationship could suffer as well.

NEUTRALS AND COLOR

A common issue I found among my clients relates to an imbalance of colors and neutrals. Most people feel drawn to color and want to surround themselves with those colors they are drawn to. However, giving those colors a neutral canvas can really help them to stand out even more. In most cases like this, the decorative elements that I usually end up bringing into my client's spaces are all neutral in tone.

Once you've got the decorative elements of your space looking balanced, it's time to focus on the energetic side. Here are some ways that you can set the tone to that of calm serenity in your space.

Different Types of Meditation

Truth be told, I myself am not a great meditator. I like guided meditations because they still give my brain something to listen to, and I also like psychic meditations like the ones in this book, which involve a lot of visualization. I need something for my conscious mind to focus on if I'm to get into a state of tranquility.

When it comes to feeling balanced and calm at home, the transitionary state between awake alertness and deep meditation is called "the alpha state." This is the feeling you have after a particularly good workout, sex, a walk in nature, or any other activity that lets your mind relax. There are lots of ways to get there, and once you become more aware of what puts you personally in this state, you can be more intentional about making it a practice. My friend Ana, for example, considers herself a shamanic witch. She is also an avid textile artist. She uses slow, steady drumbeats to help others enter the alpha state in her shamanic work, and she uses knitting to enter it herself.

A few years ago I moved into an apartment with a kitchen large enough to let me actually cook proper meals for the first time. I started teaching myself how to cook and was pleasantly surprised at how relaxing I found the process. The acts of chopping, prepping, and following a recipe puts me in a meditative state.

Meditation doesn't have to mean sitting still with your eyes closed. Some sort of traditional meditation practice is helpful, of course, but maybe there are some other things that you find relaxing and which you can make a practice out

of. Maybe for you it's yoga? Maybe it's dancing or automatic writing, drawing or painting? Putting a little intention into how you relax at home will go a long way in bringing calm and balance into your space.

Plants!

As a recovering black thumb, I can tell you that as tough as it is to keep houseplants alive, it can be very rewarding to have some fresh, green vitality in your space.

HOUSEPLANTS CAN BRING
ALL THE FOUR ELEMENTS
INTO YOUR SPACE, WHICH MAKES
THEM GREAT FOR ENHANCING
BALANCE.

The plant itself cleanses the air, the soil is earth, the light it needs is fire, and, of course, all plants need water!

HausPlants: A (Self-)Care Guide

Cheryl Rafuse, the HausWitch resident "plant protector," is here to tell us a little bit more about the magic of "HausPlants":

Stand in the woods or a garden, calm your mind, and tune into everything around you. From the rustling of leaves to the swaying sound of tall grasses, you can hear the plants around you: the creak of a pine, the snapping of an old branch. How do you feel? Calm? At peace?

These sounds, the aura of the wilderness, and those feelings are hard to come by inside a home, unless you're blessed to live in a tree house. By bringing a little nature indoors, you can change the energy of a space. When you think about it, every plant has an ancestor that lived and thrived outside. By providing them with a home you're bringing their lineage into your space and paying respect to the earth around you.

Plants help create a tiny ecosystem indoors. They have needs that make you create a better space for all living things, including people. They also bring in their own healing plant vibrations. They create oxygen and help move the energy of the space around so it doesn't feel stagnant. I also find plants in a space relaxes the eyes and mind, enhancing the feelings of being cozy and nested in your space.

PLANTS AND AURAS

Plants can raise the vibe of any space as long as it's the right match for them. When you decide to bring plants into a space you have to be sure to have the proper lighting and environment.

Do you have a sunlit spot? You could place herbs, cacti, or air plants by the window.

If you have less light you could go for an eternity plant or peace lily. It might make you think differently about a space. Do you have a dark room that no plant could live in? Are you happy there? Do you feel at ease? If you can't bring in any sunshine, does the space need a UV light? Sometimes, if you can't find a plant that will be happy in a space, you need to evaluate what else you can do to make that space feel welcoming.

PLANT MAGIC

Choosing the right plant can also mean bringing in plants with magical properties. For instance, many folks grow the money tree plant for good luck and abundance, whereas sage is cleansing, rosemary is grown for ritual and remembrance, lavender for calming anxiety, and so on. You can also choose plants symbolically. I wanted to honor elk and deer energy for their connection to spirit and the vitality they represent, but wasn't too crazy about the idea of taxidermy staring me in the face. I decided on a giant staghorn fern to represent that energy in a way that encourages growth instead of representing death.

Here are some more plants and their symbolism for inspiration. But use your intuition, and the right plant will find you.

Ivy for growing past your limitations.

Tropical plants to encourage warmth, like a rubber plant.

Cacti to represent boundaries.

Peace lily for tranquility.

Swiss cheese plant for creating space.

Boston ferns for growth.

Aloe vera for calm.

CENTERING MEDITATION

Whatever plant you choose, you have to learn what it needs.
Use your plant's watering schedule to bring order into your
own routine and to enhance your feelings of being grounded.

1

Water your plants around the same time on the same day
or days each week. Do this in the morning so the
plant has plenty of time to photosynthesize and drink all
that water throughout the hours that follow, and use
this act to set an intention for the day. Maybe you want to
focus on abundance or growth—plants are great
conduits for both. Maybe it's a pruning day: think about
things you may need to prune from your life.

2

I like to combine my tea meditation with my plant practice.
I make myself a cup of herbal tea and think about
my intentions for the day, or simply center myself and focus
on the loose herbs in the brew. After I've finished drinking
it, I take the herbal mixture and put it on the topsoil of
my plants. I do this maybe once or twice a year in the early
spring and, later, in summer. It provides my plants with
some extra nutrients and helps me feel as though I've
"planted" my most recent intentions in a very real way.

Cycles

Remember, it's necessary to be ruthless with your plants; cut off dead leaves or make the call to send them to the bin! Just know that even those of us with the greenest of thumbs have had plant friends we've had to put out to pasture.

A way to keep track of when you should be planting, growing, or trimming is to pay attention to the cycles of the moon. As the moon waxes, set your intentions and let your plants grow, plant seeds, and propagate succulents. When the moon is waning, consider what you want to let go of, declutter, and trim back your plants (if they need it!).

When plants get too big for their pots, you can carefully divide them and share parts with friends. When my cheese plant needed a bigger pot, I repotted some of the loose roots and gave the pot, along with a note of intention, to a friend who was starting a business to encourage their growth and success.

Start thinking about what kind of energy you'd like to honor in your home. Do you have a cat and want to try growing wheatgrass for your little familiar? Do you have sunlight and want to give air plants a try, to represent movement? Think about which plant might help you bring the right magic into your home.

CRYSTALS FOR BALANCE AND CALM

There are many crystals with properties that will help to balance your energy and calm your mind. The ones I've chosen to highlight here are those that can easily extend that healing into the space around you as well. Try holding them in your hand while meditating, or placing them in a high-traffic area of your space to transmute hyperactive energy to calm.

ARAGONITE

Perfect for restoring and re-centering your auric field in times of stress. It brings in star energy, which is universally healing. By clearing past emotional wounds, aragonite opens up your auric field for deep healing and exploration of your life's deeper purpose.

DOLOMITE

Brings in calm by softening emotions and neutralizing extreme moods. It can also bring awareness to the balance of giving and receiving energies in your life to aid you in making changes if necessary.

TIGER'S EYE

Taps into the primal strength of your lower body, grounding you and helping you to stand in your own power. It balances the Yin and Yang energies of the emotional body, making it easy to understand both sides of a disagreement or other divisive issue, and to find common ground in the extremes.

Aragonite

Dolomite

Tiger's eye

Now it's time to sit back, take a deep breath—
and relax! You've worked hard to make a sanctuary
out of your home and you deserve to enjoy it.

IN CLOSING

I sincerely hope that *HausMagick* has provided you with a useful framework that allows you to heal and make the very best of your space through intention-setting and magic. It has been an honor to curate the ideas and practical tips in this book for you.

The journey toward making a house feel like home is such a worthwhile pursuit, and I wish you all the best as you embark on it. Authentically connecting to your home is an essential part of self-care. Your manifested, cleared, protected, comfortable, harmonious, and balanced home will offer you a sanctuary like none other in which to connect with your highest and best self. But rather than stopping there, I hope you will be able to bring that energy out of your space and into your community, where it can have a positive influence on the world around you. In the end, this is why I love doing what I do!

Recommended Reading

Paul Beyerl, *The Master Book of Herbalism*, Phoenix Publishing, 1998

Bo Forbes, *Yoga for Emotional Balance*, Shambhala, 2011

Anna Franklin, *The Hearth Witch's Compendium: Magical and Natural Living for Every Day*, Llewellyn, 2017

John Friedlander and Gloria Hemsher, *Basic Psychic Development: A User's Guide to Auras, Chakras, and Clairvoyance*, Weiser, 2012

Malcolm Gaskill, *Witchcraft: A Very Short Introduction*, Oxford University Press, 2010

Sarah Gottesdiener, *Many Moons Workbooks*, 2016–2018

Karen Hamaker-Zondag, *Tarot as a Way of Life: A Jungian Approach to the Tarot*, Red Wheel/Weiser, 1997

Rachel Howe, *Small Spells Black & White Tarot Deck Set*, Discipline Press, smallspells.com

Robin Wall Kimmerer, *Braiding Sweetgrass: Indigenous Wisdom, Scientific Knowledge, and the Teachings of the Plants*, Milkweed Editions, 2015

Marie Kondo, *The Life-Changing Magic of Tidying Up*, Vermilion, 2014

Clare Cooper Marcus, *House as a Mirror of Self: Exploring the Deeper Meaning of Home*, Hays, 2007

Tisha Morris, *Mind, Body, Home: Transform Your Life One Room at a Time*, Llewellyn, 2014

Mandy Paradise, *Witches, Pagans, and Cultural Appropriation: Considerations & Applications for a Magical Practice*, Anchor and Star, 2017

Kristin Petrovich, *Elemental Energy: Crystal and Gemstone Rituals for a Beautiful Life*, HarperElixir, 2016

Robert Simmons, *The Pocket Book of Stones: Who They Are and What They Teach*, North Atlantic Books, 2015

Jan Spiller and Karen McCoy, *Spiritual Astrology: A Path to Divine Awakening*, Touchstone, 2010

Esther M. Sternberg, MD, *Healing Spaces: The Science of Place and Well-Being*, Harvard University Press, 2010

Andrew Theitic (ed.), *The Witches' Almanac*, Witches' Almanac Publications

Tess Whitehurst, *Magical Housekeeping: Simple Charms and Practical Tips for Creating a Harmonious Home*, Llewellyn, 2010

Contributors

CHERYL RAFUSE

Cheryl Rafuse has a green thumb—she's spent her entire life speaking to plants, researching their favorite conditions, and learning their language. She is a certified herbalist and nature lover who spends her off time as mediator between her plants and her monodactyle black cat in Salem, Massachusetts. Cheryl is HausWitch's manager/plant protector and runs a marketing and copywriting business called Howl Content. Follow her on Instagram @witcheryl and work with her at howlcontent.com.

LAUREN HALL

Lauren Hall lives in a 313-year-old haunted house just outside of Salem. When she's not making friends with her resident ghosts (or, let's face it, stripping wallpaper), she's often helping other people with spirit communication.

SHAINA COHEN

Shaina Cohen is a geologist who received her MSc from Boston College in 2016. During this time, she studied the deformation of olivine crystals sourced from Earth's mantle. Her greatest passions include being a rock hound, teaching about the wonders of Earth Science, and encouraging young minds to become involved in STEM fields. You can find Shaina on Instagram @shainagram.

GRACE HARRINGTON MURDOCH

Grace Harrington Murdoch, creatrix of Flowers & Stars essential oil and flower essence blends, is a flower essence practitioner, astrologer, and author of the book *Child Awake*. She has been studying healing and astrology for over ten years. She has had a busy private practice since 2009, where she teaches and provides Reiki, polarity therapy, astrology, crystal healing, and more. With Venus on her Midheaven (career point), she loves to explore the relationship between art, love, beauty, storytelling, and astrology. She loved contributing to the Moon in the fourth house chapter! You can reach her for in-person or distance readings at flowersandstars.org and on Instagram @flowersandstars_.

MADELINE MOONEY

Madeline Mooney is a Reiki master, herbalist, and intuitive with a strong connection to the natural realm. She uses intuitive channeling to support communication with animals. Connect with Madeline via her website moonchildreikiandherbals.com or follow her on Instagram @moonchild.reikiandherbals.

JESSICA JONES LAVOIE

Jessica Jones Lavoie is an energy worker, maker of wall spells, mother, and cocreator of LightHaus magical cleaning products. She earned her degree in environmental geology from Salem State University and has been a practicing Usui Reiki Master Teacher since 2013. She loves to share her blend of science and Spirit to empower others to heal themselves, the land, and water. You can find her singing to the ocean, leading moon meditations, and holding private healing sessions at the HausWitch Healing Space or on Instagram @evolving.light.

MELISSA NIERMAN

Melissa Nierman is the founder of NOW Age Travel, a modern metaphysical travel company in Salem, Massachusetts. She's a tarot educator, Reiki practitioner, and intrepid tour guide with a masters in education. She cofacilitates a monthly community Tarot Salon at the HausWitch store, leads hands-on Tarot Journey walking workshops, and teaches Tarot for Lovers classes. She's also the author of *Tarot for Lovers: A Workbook for Exploring All Kinds of Magical Relationships*. Find her at nowagetravel.com and @now.age.

MICHAELA ZULLO

Originally from Youngstown, Ohio, Michaela Zullo was drawn to Salem over a decade ago. She graduated from Salem State University with a bachelors of science in geology. Combining her knowledge of the earth with her passion for intuitive healing practices, she has cultivated an understanding of many natural systems.

LAKSHMI RAMGOPAL

Lakshmi Ramgopal is a writer, historian, and musician who holds a PhD in classics from the University of Chicago. Lakshmi's academic research examines colonialism and identity. She brings these concepts to bear on white communities' practice of magic with the phrase "responsible witchcraft," which she coined to address and provide solutions for dealing with cultural appropriation and racism. You can find her at http://LakshmiR.com and @lykanthea.

Acknowledgments

First and foremost, I'd like to thank everyone who has supported HausWitch over the years. To all of you who have read the blog, visited the store, or followed on social media, I am so incredibly grateful that it's hard to find the right words. You are the true magic of my life.

Thank you to Laura Higginson and the team at Penguin Random House/Ebury for your interest, vision, and patience.

Thank you so much to Anna Paustenbach, Mary Duke, Lisa Zuniga, Courtney Nobile, and the whole team at HarperOne for giving *HausMagick* the perfect home here in the US. And endless thanks to Meg Thompson for swooping in and saving so many days with her kindness and literary witchcraft.

To my love and partner in everything, Melissa Nierman, thank you for seeing me and challenging me and bringing cosmic joy and light into my life.

To my coven of collaborators: Grace Harrington Murdoch, Lauren Hall, Jessica Jones Lavoie, Madeline Mooney, Cheryl Rafuse, Maggie Smith, Michaela Zullo, Shaina Cohen, Erika Leahey, Winnie Man, Ariel Cefalo, Kaitlyn Soligan, Sailaja Ganti Joshi, SriVani Yerramilli, and Lakshmi Ramgopal. Thank you for the myriad ways that you have made this book richer and more inspired.

To all the amazing makers whose art fills the pages of this book: Rachel Howe, Christina Kosinski, Leela Hoehn Robinson, Julia Canright, Marisa Curran, Daniel Zender, and Claire Nereim. I will forever be in awe and jealous of your talents.

Thank you to Lauren and Michael Berkowitz, Morgan Elliot and Jordan Awan, and Grace and Peter Harrington Murdoch for allowing me to photograph your homes and bring HausMagick to life.

Thank you to Lindsay Kelly for making this book look better than my dreams.

To my mother, Sharon Feldmann, thank you for teaching me to bake, and to craft and make seven-foot-tall palm trees out of PVC tubing and papier-mâché.

Special thanks to Dawn Livorsi for taking me under your wing, to Dave Wells for always carrying the heavy stuff, and to Christopher Rhodes for always knowing.

ABOUT ERICA

Owner and founder of HausWitch Erica Feldmann has been using intuition to heal spaces from a very young age. A Chicago native, Erica moved to Salem, Massachusetts, in 2010 to study witches and the sacred feminine in the Gender and Cultural Studies graduate program at Simmons College. The knowledge she gained there, combined with her innate talent for interiors, came together to form HausWitch, a company devoted to helping people heal their spaces and love their homes. Decorating her clients' homes on shoestring budgets taught her about the challenges people confront in their homes and habitats. Opened in 2015, the HausWitch shop is a manifestation of her dream that all people should have a little magic in their homes. Erica now lives in downtown Salem in a magical haus with her two cats and her wife.

Index

A SPELL IS JUST A PRAYER
WITH PROPS